*Readings on the Nature
of History and the Problems of
Historical Interpretation*

EDITED BY

THOMAS N. GUINSBURG

The
DIMENSIONS
of History

& Company
CHICAGO

D
6
.G84
1971
Oct.1998

PREFACE

Too often students plunge into introductory history courses knowing little about the nature of history and the problems of historical interpretation. By placing a consideration of these matters before beginning students, this collection of readings aims to help undergraduates overcome that lack of understanding. The selections are by no means comprehensive. Perhaps they will raise more questions than they will answer, and that may be all to the good.

Reading and reflecting on these selections should help a student stop regarding history as a fixed and final commodity found between the covers of a textbook, if he has not already done so. The first section discusses everyone's need to develop a capacity for reading history critically. The second group of readings offers a student samples of divergent points of view on the nature of history. The final section illustrates the varied forces one must consider in assessing reasons for historical change.

Altogether, the readings are intended to provide insight into the complexity of historical study. They should lead a student to recognize that understanding history requires critical intelligence, sensitivity, and imagination—not merely a retentive memory. If he studies history with this in mind, the benefits will be appreciable. He not only will find his course more challenging and exciting; hopefully he will leave it with a capacity for analysis and perception —and an awareness of the richness of human experience—that will serve him well long after most of the names and dates have been forgotten.

Thomas N. Guinsburg

ACKNOWLEDGMENTS

I am greatly indebted to the history faculty and first-year students at the University of Western Ontario for their help with this project. Several colleagues were generous in their encouragement and perceptive in criticizing an earlier version of the book. The students in History 20, after using that version, responded with alacrity to an invitation to offer comments. Both groups deserve thanks for adding to the book's merits; neither should be blamed for the remaining shortcomings. John Morgan brought intelligence and energy to the role of research assistant. Ted Tieken of Rand McNally and Jim Clark were most congenial and helpful editors.

T.N.G.

Table of Contents

On History: Some Conflicting Comments

A nation which does not know what it was yesterday, does not know what it is today, nor what it is trying to do.

—WOODROW WILSON

Peoples and governments have never learned anything from history, or acted on principles deducible from it.

—G. W. F. HEGEL

Historical knowledge is not a variety of knowledge, but it is knowledge itself; it is the form which completely fills and exhausts the field of knowing.... —BENEDETTO CROCE

History is only a confused heap of facts.

—GILBERT KEITH CHESTERTON

History is indeed the witness of the times, the light of truth.

—CICERO

If a man could say nothing against a character but what he can prove, history could not be written.

—SAMUEL JOHNSON

History is simply a piece of paper covered with print; the main thing is still to make history, not to write it.

—OTTO VON BISMARCK

Anybody can make history; only a great man can write it.

—OSCAR WILDE

Universal history, the history of what man has accomplished in this world, is at bottom the History of the Great Men who have worked here. —THOMAS CARLYLE

No single man makes history. History cannot be seen, just as one cannot see grass growing. —BORIS PASTERNAK

History is a science, no less and no more. —J. B. BURY

The historian can learn much from the novelist.

—SAMUEL ELIOT MORISON

1

I.
The Challenges
of History

INTRODUCTION

Consciously or not, all men perform as historians. Each of us makes judgments and decisions based on his knowledge, however inadequate, of what has gone before. Hence to "take" history as a course is not, as the following selection points out, an enterprise totally divorced from one's day-to-day concerns. "A sensible man," wrote Sophocles, "judges of present by past events." If this is so, then understanding the nature of historical study provides not simply a key to success in a classroom. More important, it becomes a means of enhancing one's capacity as a human being, for the intelligence and sensitivity with which we act in the present depend, at least in part, on the perspectives we draw from the past.

Beware, however, of overemphasizing the immediate utility of history. Although men as far back as Confucius have claimed that studying the past enables one to foretell the future, even those historians proudest of their skills rarely list prophecy among them. As for understanding the present, if Hegel's pronouncement that "peoples and governments have never learned anything from history" strikes us as overly cynical, it is not altogether unfounded. Other men, including many of the authors whose works are here assembled, have rightly insisted that the "lessons" of history are elusive and ambiguous even to those who seek them. Students who look to history for facile forecasts of the future or for easy answers to present problems search in vain.

Study of the past, if not the source of all wisdom, can nonetheless offer rich bounties. Beholding the human pageant in times and places far and near can be sheer pleasure. Finding this sufficient gratification, many professional historians bemoan the task of justifying in other ways the craft they unhesitatingly pursue for intellectual and aesthetic delight. But students these days, while hoping for enjoyment from their courses, are rightly seeking more. Disenchanted with history courses stressing the memorization of minutiae, many demand that a course challenge minds, broaden horizons and, to use a current watchword, be "relevant."

This book explores the challenges and vistas of historical study. Though from time to time the editor and the authors of the selections deal with the direct relevance of historical knowledge, throughout they discuss history as a sophisticated discipline that sharpens awareness and broadens vision. Such qualities, presumably, are scarcely irrelevant to the concerns of men and women in the 1970's.

How can the study of history bestow these attributes? First, it liberates us from what Lord Acton called the "tyranny of environment." It provides a world outside the personal frame of reference which, for better or worse, has conditioned an individual's experiences. What Arnold Toynbee has written about the value of a classical education might well be applied to the study of history. "It has given me," he notes, "a mental standing-ground outside the time and place into which I happen to have been born." All men need such a "mental standing-ground" outside their own time in order to be more perceptive observers within it.

No one, moreover, can understand his own society without comprehending its evolution. History will not explain everything about the current state of affairs, but it will infuse sense into many matters otherwise bewildering. Perplexities about the contemporary world will persist—our own epoch, indeed, abounds in novelty. All the more reason, though, to seek out the past's perspectives, which show that if our own era is unique, so are all eras. If ours is an age of turbulent change, others no less turbulent have preceded it. If this generation faces complex problems, previous generations have confronted similar complexities. "In times of change," John Dos Passos has written, "when there is a quicksand of fear under men's reasoning, a sense of continuity with generations gone before can stretch like a lifeline across the scary present."

History, then, can be a source of consolation in a bewildering

4

world. Yet unless we are careful, it may also prove an opiate, lulling us to accept present institutions and policies because "history" indicates that they are best and wisest. Perhaps certain institutions do have unassailable historical foundations; perhaps lessons from history do sustain present policies. On the other hand, perhaps they do not. How can one tell, unless his own comprehension of history is sufficiently sophisticated and mature? This, in part, is George Kitson Clark's message in the selection below. History is invoked all around us, sometimes very subtly. Consequently, by studying history carefully, we defend ourselves against those who, purposefully or not, use history toward particular ends that may not please us.

Few students of history will become professional historians. Yet many may serve as teachers, most as parents, all as participants in their society. The fulfillment of each of these roles demands serious study of the past. The "facts" of history, as the second section of this book points out, do not speak for themselves. A person must learn to interpret these facts himself or passively accept the evaluations of others. The best history courses, therefore, offer their students not merely specific interpretations but, more important, opportunities to develop the ability to make them. If uncritical acceptance may sometimes do an individual no immediate harm, it may well bring ruin to a society. George Orwell's grim vision of a totally manipulated culture in 1984 underscores the necessity of free and serious historical inquiry.

Historians try to provide the materials by which their readers can gain an unshackled understanding of man's heritage and potential. Studying these materials, to repeat, may not insure wisdom or progress, but it should help to preclude those defects of perception and vision that impair freedom of choice. The great British historian F. W. Maitland summed it up well: "Today we study the day before yesterday, in order that yesterday may not paralyse today, and today may not paralyse tomorrow." What challenge could be greater?

GEORGE KITSON CLARK (b. 1900), a British historian specializing in studies of England in the nineteenth century, has written a most penetrating and lucid introduction to historical study, *The Critical Historian.* In that book, an excerpt from which follows, he expresses his firm belief that "every man or woman is confronted with a great deal of history every day of their lives." What dangers, according to Dr. Kitson Clark, may befall the person who fails to study history carefully? What qualities does he find essential to mature historical understanding?

The Critical Historian

History is the record of what has happened in the past, of anything that has ever happened in the past, however long ago or however recently. It is sometimes suggested that what seems to be trivial is "unworthy of the dignity of history," or that the account of what happened in the last few years "cannot yet be called history." In fact there is a tendency to confine the word "history" to what can be put into a serious history book, and perhaps taught with safety and without controversial overtones in schools and colleges. It is a tendency much to be deplored. It is better to accept, as an axiom, the definition that any attempt to describe what has happened before the actual moment of narration shall be called history, for that carries with it the corollary that every such attempt presents some of the problems which are common to all historical work, and therefore may be subjected to the same critical technique as that to which history books are subjected. . . .

So defined, history is a commodity in almost universal use. Gossip which makes any attempt to describe something which really took place must be called history. All business transactions depend on some form of history; so do all cases at law. All scientific results must depend on a rather specialized form of history. All journalism

From Chapters 1, 2, 10 of *The Critical Historian* by George Kitson Clark (London: Heinemann Educational Publishers, 1967; New York: Basic Books, 1967). Reprinted with permission of the author and the publishers.

7

is an attempt to write history. Politics and the affairs of state cannot be understood without a knowledge of the immediate history of the transactions which are going forward, of the situation from which those transactions emerged and of the historical background before which all is enacted.

Indeed it is because of the importance of this background that the influence of history is so pervasive, and historians have such great opportunities to do good or evil. How pervasive this historical background is may perhaps be best realized through the way it affects the meaning, and colour, of words in common use. Take two words which might easily affect the same important modern argument, *barbarism* and *colonialism*. Each implies an epitome of past history, each possibly an explanation of it, each perhaps a generalization about it. *Barbarism* summarizes the mode of life which it is believed has characterized primitive nations, *Colonialism* the aggressive policy which it is said has too often been followed by more advanced ones. A variety of explanations are possible both of the mode of life of the one group and of the policy of the other. Each depends upon a particular reading of history. It may be held that barbarians have behaved barbarously because this was inherent in the stock from which they sprang, or alternatively that they happened to be situated away from the highway of human progress and had no chance to do otherwise. It may be held that colonialist annexation was a natural, in some cases a defensible, even in some cases an unavoidable, policy for the colonialist powers at certain epochs in the world's history; or alternatively that it was always an aberration to which the colonialist powers were driven either by something that was inherently evil in their nature, or by the ambition and greed of their ruling classes.

As men's interpretations of history differ so will their views about what policy should be followed in future. If barbarous nations have been barbarous because it was their nature so to be, then, if they become independent, they will slowly or quickly sink back into barbarism, and it is no good acting on the assumption that they will do anything else. If their barbarism was the result of historic chance, then they are likely to be capable of moving forward with reasonable speed into a full independent civilized life. If the occupation of the territory by the colonial power was wholly indefensible, the wicked work of evil men, then perhaps everything that springs from it must be eliminated. If, however, the occupation was a natural phase through which both nations passed, and the motives of those to whom it gave control were possibly good, or partly good, then the colony may have inherited from it much that it will do well to keep when the connection has come to an end.

All this can be implied by the use of these words, and all of it, interpretations and conclusions, implies the making of a number of generalizations about difficult and often little known history. Even the use of the words at all implies fairly wide historical assumptions, for the different actions which are labelled with the words *barbarism* and *colonialism* may be so various that they cannot properly be grouped under one term, and the sense and implications of either word may be wholly misleading with regard to some of them.

Even when a word is more exact in its meaning, when it is in fact a term of art drawn from an abstract argument, it may have overtones which come from assumptions about history, and it is quite likely that it is these overtones which determine the force of its emotional impact. The word *capitalism* can no doubt be defined in the terms of reasonably strict economic analysis, yet it gains its colour very largely from what people believe capitalist society has been like. Or alternatively the words *communism* or *socialism* are words which strictly used should stand for various theories of the way in which society should be organized, but they are constantly used by people who have only the vaguest knowledge of the theories in question, but believe that they know, for good or ill, how socialists or communists have behaved. It is on that knowledge that their emotional reactions to the words are based.

If this is true of words which stand for abstractions it is likely to be still more true of the names of the great historic entities which have come down through a longer and more varied past. The words *German, Catholic* and *Jew* stand respectively for a nation, a Church and a race. They are used to describe things which exist in the world today, and therefore men's reaction to them should presumably be conditioned by what they are now. In fact, however, in each case men's reactions are largely affected by memories of history, or what passes for history, which seems to disclose the nature of Germans, or Jews, or Roman Catholics in their actions. As the selections of history which different people remember and the versions of history which different people accept will be by no means the same, so their reactions to them will differ, sometimes very violently.

Sometimes a quite ordinary word will be caught up into the current of history and receive a new significance. A good example of this is the word *appeasement*. Its dictionary meanings are colourless, but in the years immediately before 1939 it became attached to a particular policy, and gained a new meaning in the vocabulary of politics which can cause strong emotional reactions. Others gain a colour from having served as the jargon of past controversies and so come to seem to have a clearer meaning than on analysis they possess; such words for instance as *Aryan, decadent* and possibly *reactionary*.

Yet though all these words gain their power from their association from history it is not necessary that the history which gives this power should have ever been systematically studied, or be very clearly remembered by those who are influenced by them. Some of their associations may have been derived from confusedly remembered lessons learnt at school, some inculcated by the reiterated assertions of politicians. Some associations survive from misty recollections of newspaper controversies, from scraps of special information or of personal experience, or the stories of chance acquaintances. The clear pictures of historical situations or of characters provided by historical novels or films, particularly those seen in youth, often seem to leave a curiously lasting impression. The reactions of a fair number of people in a past generation towards the Roman Catholic Church were probably, at least in part, affected by the novels of Charles Kingsley, possibly endorsed by a picture of the massacre of St. Bartholomew drawn from the novels of Stanley Weyman. Yet, while on the one hand the entertainments of boyhood or girlhood seem sometimes to leave a deep impression, on the other, to an extent which is humiliating to schoolmasters and dons, the history which should have been learnt systematically in school or college seems often to have taken so little root that intelligent and apparently highly educated adults are curiously at the mercy of very questionable historical generalizations and descriptions against which any normal historical education should have guarded them.

From this haphazard mass of misty knowledge, scraps of information, fiction in fancy dress and hardly conscious historical memories is woven a network of historical associations which stretches over the whole field of human consciousness. Thus words are converted into spells, symbols are endowed with emotional force and stereotypes emerge which pretend to describe whole groups of people, and predict from their past their probable conduct in the future. Here in fact are some of the most powerful forces which control the human mind. They are of much use to those who wish to invoke irrational loyalties; they are also of great value to those who wish to use and to direct the emotion of hatred.

It is for this reason that the work of the historian can be turned into a propaganda weapon of great power. It can exhibit and enforce existing prejudices, and it can create new ones. Probably most people are more easily and more powerfully moved by the accounts of concrete events than by the rehearsal of abstract generalizations, and the historian can normally turn up suitable incidents and recount them vividly. Stories of heroism, or stories of oppression, or best of all stories of martyrdom which combine the pathos of oppression and the glory of heroism will make the heart beat faster and strongly enforce the desired political or religious prejudices, particularly if it is thought to be wrong to consider the case from the point of view of the other side and right to forget the martyrdoms which one's own friends may have inflicted on other people.

Behind this, endorsed by this concrete detail, is the picture of the world which the historian may paint, portraying certain nations and classes as being habitually in the wrong and working evil, while other nations are immaculate, heroic and normally their victims. Behind this again are the general theories of human behaviour, which are held to determine the conditions under which all life is lived for each of which, whatever they are, the historian can usually supply conclusive evidence.

The influence of history may therefore be great, and may be wholly evil. It can be used by the self-deceived or by the plain liar, it can be used by the fanatic or by the propagandist, it can excite passions which lead to hatred and so to human violence and misery. It engenders the venom which makes wars likely. How dangerous the abuses of misapplied history may be, the record of the last half-century in Europe, particularly in Germany, amply testifies, and, unless the human race is unusually lucky, no doubt the record of the next half-century, particularly in parts of Asia and of Africa, will confirm.

Yet dangerous as these historical entanglements are it is not easy to see a way of escape. A man cannot escape from history by simply saying that he will disregard it, and will fix his eyes firmly on the present. To disregard the past is very often the surest means of becoming its slave. A man who ignores history will still make the historical assumptions which are implicit in most language and in all political judgements, but he will not know he is making them and so will be unable to criticize them or reconsider the evidence on which they are based. Nor is it possible to escape the great historical controversies which split politics and shake the world. If a man takes the Olympian view, which attracts so many people, that there is always much to be said for both sides in any controversy, and that therefore the truth must lie about half-way between the extremes, he will play himself straight into the hands of the least responsible of the contestants; for the more extravagant are the statements made the more certainly will the middle position be drawn to the side of those who make them. Nor is there a possible retreat into what purports to be a careless universal scepticism such as commends itself to the sophisticated. Such a scepticism is stupid because it is blind and can never be complete. A man must believe something, and the fact that he has summarily rejected a great many things which other people believe is no guarantee that he is able to criticize whatever it is that he himself accepts.

There is only one way to escape. It is laborious, frustrating and uncertain: but there is no alternative. What has to be done is not to disregard history, but to use it more effectively. Perhaps the first thing to be done is, as far as possible, to get clear in one's own mind what historical conclusions the language, the political creeds, the programmes and the propaganda of the moment assume. When this has been done, clearly the next task should be to consider upon what evidence such conclusions must rest if they are to be believed and whether such evidence is likely to be available and to be reliable. All this may have a wholesome purgative effect. A certain number of the historical assumptions which are made by political propagandists or implied in common political jargon when clearly postulated can be seen to be not credible, or even if they are credible there can still be no reason to believe them, for the evidence which would be needed to substantiate them could never be produced.

Such a negative result is of course valuable. If men have learnt to doubt what they ought to doubt clearly something valuable has been achieved. But as clearly it would be both frustrating and dangerous if that was all that could be done, if after the nonsense had been dissipated all that was left was so uncertain and evasive that no man could risk using it as a basis for his beliefs and calculations. There is a well known danger in being empty, swept and garnished. Every man needs some conception of the past upon which he can rely if he is to talk about the present or plan for the future, and if no clear conceptions are vouchsafed him by critical scholarship he will get them from elsewhere.

Fortunately there should be no need for him to do that. Great difficulties stand in the way of establishing the complete and unquestionable truth about anything, but it is seldom difficult to establish something nearer the truth than what is generally believed. Certainly the evidence is always more doubtful, or equivocal, or incomplete than is normally obvious to the casual observer, and it should be accepted as an axiom that motives are always a matter for speculation. Worst of all, all investigators are human and, being human, are liable to bias. Nevertheless against all this should be placed the positive achievements of historical scholarship particularly since the development of historical method began in the last century. Since then, indeed from long before then, historical scholars have tried to develop methods which will enable them to extract as much truth as possible from the evidence available and a tradition which will eliminate as far as possible the influence of personal bias from their work. In neither task have they been completely successful, nor can they be. In many important historical enquiries absolute certainty is not to be obtained, the evidence will not supply it; and bias of one sort or another is protean and all pervasive, no man is free from it. Nevertheless it can be said with some confidence that in very many matters the labours of scholars have produced a version of history which is a better guide to what really happened, a more secure basis for thought and action than those versions which usually confirm political credulity and supply material for propaganda.

Even so no version of history ought to be believed without question. No historian should be trusted implicitly. If it were possible it would be desirable to learn something of a historian's personality and preoccupations in order to be able to check his bias; that would however be often tedious and often impracticable, for the lives and personalities of many scholars are necessarily and properly lost in an unmemorable past. In all cases, however,

13

the work should be considered critically in relation to the evidence which it purports to use, and if it is accepted it should be accepted tentatively not as something definitive, but as a workable hypothesis, which may be modified or replaced in due course by the further work of scholarship and the accumulation of new evidence.

To adopt this attitude, to effect these criticisms or even to know what criticisms might be relevant requires training. Much of it is not very difficult training. Much indeed consists in learning to ask of any report certain simple questions, the purport of which is obvious as soon as they are described. In addition to this it is probably desirable to study the methods of certain historians, sometimes to learn what should be done and sometimes to learn what should not be done and to be shewn the pitfalls into which many intelligent men have fallen. In most cases what has to be mastered are the obvious and easily forgotten lessons of commonsense. It is true that historians do use specialized techniques, but they can confidently be left to the specialists who use them, though it is interesting to know of their existence. But though this training in historical criticism should not be difficult it is suggested that it might give to any man or woman who has received it something of great value, the realization of how much, or how little, they can expect to know about matters of importance and possibly the capacity to criticize the evidence on which the dangerous legends or myths of the world may be supposed to be founded, or at least to see how it might be criticized.

If there is truth in this it would seem to be important that the habits of historical criticism should be developed from the moment anyone begins to take an intelligent interest in history, or for that matter in current affairs. This means that children should be introduced to the study in their later years at school, particularly those children who are specializing in history, but not only those children since these techniques are for general use. This would be incompatible with the dogmatic way in which in the past history used too often to be taught. Sometimes, even in the not too remote past, the facts of history, neatly tabulated with their causes carefully enumerated, were rationed out to those whose privilege it was to learn but not to argue, to be accepted because the teacher said so or because they were to be found in that authoritative oracle "the book," whatever book it was that the school was using or examiners had prescribed. It was a method which never satisfied the best

14

teachers, and, it may be guessed, is very little used now. Nowadays there is freer discussion of historical issues, a much greater use of original material, and it is suggested that there might be a wider discussion of the problems presented by the use of evidence both by the historians who write history books and the historians who write for the daily newspaper....

A framework of unquestionable fact covers, after some sort, a large area of human affairs. Unless for some philosophical reason all knowledge is uncertain, the knowledge of these facts is certain. It has never covered the whole field of human affairs, and as you go further back into history the spaces in the latticework get larger. Though the main members of the framework are by definition unquestionable it must always be a matter of dispute and judgement how far it extends, and there are also in the history of any period disputable facts, likely guesses and probable hypotheses about facts which are not sustained by it.

The nature of human motive can never be guaranteed by the framework of fact, nor probably can the results of human action or of events, since it is not possible to know with certainty what would have happened if the facts had not been as they were. Nor is it possible to be sure that you know, or at least you know completely the causes of things. For this reason the framework of fact will never by itself supply the interpretation of history, though any interpretation that disregards the framework of fact can itself be disregarded.

Into the consideration of anything which lies beyond the framework of fact the human element will intrude. This is obvious in relation to any question of interpretation, but it is also true of any question of disputed fact. It will be necessary to take into account the extent and limitations of the powers of human beings to observe, to form inferences from what they observe, to remember, to record, to present what they have recorded in a newspaper or history book. But not only will the powers of human beings to observe, infer and record be in question, but also the ways in which they do these things will be controlled by their wills, by their passions, by their interests and by the very fact that they are human beings.

All this will produce uncertainty, but there will be degrees of uncertainty. The question with what degree of uncertainty a fact should be accepted will provide problems to be resolved by the use of trained judgement and the teaching of an experience of the problems which history presents. That judgement and experience will without doubt suggest that much of what human beings accept as part of their picture of the past is spurious, or doubtful, or unknowable. But they will also suggest descriptions and explanations of historical events which, though tentative and hypothetical, are probably a better guide to reality, and a surer basis for action, than what is proposed by the confidence of ignorance.

Unfortunately it is not normally possible for the ordinary user of history to press home himself the questions which ought to be asked of evidence into which the human element has introduced this element of uncertainty, or to resolve the problems which history presents. He may not have the skill and experience to do these things; he will probably not have the leisure; he will almost certainly not have command of the necessary material. Yet it is of considerable importance that he should understand the rudiments of historical criticism. He is after all the consumer. It is for his use that history and journalism is written. If he demands a high critical standard in what is written for him he will in the end get it. If he objects that questions have not been asked of the evidence which should have been asked, in due course those who are in a position to ask such questions will make it their business to do so.

In order to press home his legitimate requirements it is however necessary for the ordinary reader to learn more than he normally knows today about the techniques of scholarship even if he is not going to use them. For instance it is important that more ordinary unprofessional readers should understand the significance of footnotes than now seem to do so. Footnotes are not as many people seem to think the mere exuberance of pedantry, and they ought not to be, as they sometimes are, the tiresome reflections of an exhibitionist desire to parade erudition, or the result of an incurable diffuseness of mind. They should indicate, and when they are properly constructed they do indicate, the necessary links between the work of the historian and the evidence upon which it is based. Even if a reader has no chance to turn back to any of the documents cited he can learn much by letting his eye run over the footnotes of a work he is reading. He can see what kind of evidence the author is using to substantiate the statements he is making, whether it is someone's memoirs, a diary, private letters, public documents or whatever else it may be. He may guess whether his sources are likely to be one-sided, whether for instance he is taking his evidence too exclusively from the letters of one man and his circle, whether he is relying too much on obvious gossip and perhaps whether he is going back to original documents or whether he is relying on edited collections the accuracy of which may be questioned; and he may even form an opinion whether a reference can support the conclusions based on it. But none of these things can be learnt by a reader who has never learnt what a footnote is intended to do, and the rules which it ought to observe. Unfortunately many people, to judge by their comments, regard a formal footnote at the bottom of a page as a tiresome intrusion at which they have trained their eyes not to look, and are pleased when the notes are placed at the end of a book where they need not bother about them.

Scholarly writing demands scholarly reading and scholarly readers. Scholarly readers will demand a higher standard of scholarship in what is written for them, and higher standards of scholarship probably means a nearer approach to truth on matters which may be of considerable importance to mankind. But more important than any grasp of scholarly technique is the lesson of the habit of scholarly hesitation, the habit of the mind which teaches the great difficulty, even the impossibility, of arriving at the truth about many of the facts relating to events in the past. It is a habit of mind which leads to the rejection of much, and possibly the assured acceptance of little, but it can be used to dissolve forever some of the legends, the dogmatic statements, the facile explanations which have troubled mankind.

Therefore the lesson of historical criticism as applied to the facts of history is to a large extent a lesson in how to doubt what perhaps might have been accepted previously without question. But it teaches doubt, not scepticism, an uncertainty about what is to be accepted as truth, not a belief that anything might be true or that everything may be false or that knowledge is impossible. The exercise of historical criticism does not teach blind doubt, doubt that does not discriminate between the degrees of certainty and probability, but rather trained or skilled doubt, that has learnt from man's experience to make this discrimination.

To learn how to doubt should therefore be one of the important rewards of an historical education. It is one key to what should characterize the attitude of the critical historian. . . .

No man can escape from history or for long ignore it. There

is no lock to anyone's back door. Whether he likes it or not the results of history, or what purport to be the results of history, or opinions coloured by beliefs about history, will invade his life and mind. He must also be prepared for opinions about history or historical experience to have deeply affected the mind of anyone with whom he has dealings. This being so it is the act of a wise man to come to terms with what he cannot evade, and bring it, if he can, under control; that is he must try to get as near as he can to the reality in the history with which he is confronted, to test the cogency of the historical opinions which are likely to influence his mind, or the minds of anyone who is important to him, and perhaps winnow some of the nonsense out of them. It is my case that to do this he must become a *critical historian.* . . .

II.
The Nature
of History

INTRODUCTION

Debate over the question "what is history?" seems endless. Virtually every attempt to answer the question has produced a different response. Yet out of the morass of definitions and descriptions have emerged two basic "sides" in the enduring controversy.

One contends that though the historian lacks the scientist's methods of verification, he can nonetheless write "scientific" history. Such history would shun judgments about the past and simply record, in the famous phrase of the German historian Leopold von Ranke, "what actually happened" (*wie es eigentlich gewesen*). Believers in a science of history assert, moreover, that the historian can ultimately arrive at laws of human behavior analogous to laws that govern the physical universe. The converse position—expressed most elegantly in the writings of Carl Becker, author of the second reading in this section—stresses that the historian, inevitably limited in knowledge, biased, and selective in recounting the "facts" of the past, does not and cannot convey what actually happened. Instead, the historical account is but an image of the past as a particular historian sees it.

Confidence in the notion of scientific history has waned since the beginning of the twentieth century, when J. B. Bury made the address excerpted below. In 1894 the president of the American Historical Association contended that four out of five historians then alive had in the course of their work "felt that they stood on the brink of a great generalization that would reduce all history under a law as clear as the laws which govern the physical world." Probably an exaggeration even then, such a statement surely would not describe members of the historical profession today. Yet neither do most historians lapse into total despair about the prospects for making history more objective. Few would agree that accepting an interpretation amounts to what one historian has termed "an act of faith."

The debate goes on, and each student, as he ponders the readings in this section, must come to his own conclusions about the nature of historical writing. Even if he dismisses the apostles of scientific history as somewhat naive, or the "relativists" as overly skeptical, he should recognize that the conflict of opinion cannot be ignored. For it explains a great deal: why some historians have scoffed at the notion that imagination and artistry are proper characteristics of historical accounts; why others sneer at the term historical objectivity; and, especially, why one noted scholar, Pieter Geyl, has called history "an argument without end."

When reflecting on their discipline today, most historians seek to reconcile the dream of objectivity with the reality that they are neither omniscient observers of the past nor superhuman. If scientific laws of human behavior seem beyond the historian's grasp, he can nonetheless conduct a painstaking search for evidence and explore alternative explanations for events. In addition, he can employ techniques that make the best use of available materials. As Stephan Thernstrom's article points out, the modern historian striving for analytical precision can sometimes benefit from using a computer. But factual mastery, patience, and technical skill do not alone account for a historian's prowess. None of these eliminates the "human equation" from historical craftsmanship. "Each historian," J. H. Hexter notes, "brings to the rewriting of history the full range of the remembered experience of his own days, that unique array that he alone possesses and is." Helpful as this observation is, it prompts yet another question about the nature of history: what sorts of experiences promote the best historical writing?

It would be audacious to prescribe a set of experiences for students of history. But since they are observing the life of the past in its full dimensions, broad acquaintance with the many facets of human existence will help. Such familiarity, though, might stem from reading as well as direct experience, from reflection as well as interaction. Historians may well choose different paths to understanding humanity. The real question here, then, is the degree to which the scholar at work should strive to insulate himself, that is, to divorce his analysis of the past from his attitudes toward the present.

It is a widely accepted axiom that the interpreter of history should undertake his work in a spirit of detachment. Seeking to understand rather than judge the past, he should exclude his own political, social, and moral views from his historical account. Only in this manner, presumably, can the scholar succeed in making reasonably objective assessments and avoid pleading special causes. Although most historians have doubted the possibility of real detachment, the majority have nonetheless considered it a worthy goal. Others, however, have denounced disengaging past from present as not only utopian but immoral. Recently a group of "radical" historians have urged their colleagues to become deeply involved in their own times and to use the past as a means of illuminating the present, particularly its faults.

The three historians whose writings conclude this section differ in their conceptions of the nature and purposes of historical writing. Professors Hexter, Schlesinger, and Lynd probably would not define the historian's quest in identical fashion. Certainly they pursue it differently. The first seeks to disengage his professional work from his responses to the contemporary world. The other two, however dissimilar, have interwoven careers as writers and makers of history. Moreover, though each aims at providing present and future generations with deeper understanding of the past, they all seem to disagree about the goals their work should serve.

Diversity is the splendor of history. Students need not perceive its nature nor interpret its episodes identically. They will pursue its mysteries from vastly dissimilar perspectives. Yet, however they define and approach history, they should derive from its study greater critical discernment and sensitivity. On this goal "scientists" and "artists," "activists" and "bystanders" can unite.

Few historians have ever delivered a stronger or more confident plea for a science of history than **J. B. BURY** (1861–1927). A specialist in the history of the Roman Empire, he chose the occasion of his inauguration in 1903 as Regius Professor of Modern History at Cambridge to lecture on "The Science of History," excerpts from which are here reprinted. How did Bury differentiate between the type of history he applauded and the type he deplored? Why, as he admits, did many historians hesitate to view their discipline as he did? Why, two generation later, have historians not yet succeeded in writing scientific history?

The Science of History

It may be appropriate and useful now and again to pay a sort of solemn tribute to the dignity and authority of a great discipline or science, by reciting some of her claims and her laws, or by reviewing the measures of her dominion; and on this occasion, in this place, it might perhaps seem to be enough to honour the science of history in this formal way, sprinkling, as it were, with dutiful hands some grains of incense on her altar.

Yet even such a tribute might possess more than a formal significance, if we remember how recently it is—within three generations, three short generations—that history began to forsake her old irresponsible ways and prepared to enter into her kingdom. In the story of the nineteenth century, which has witnessed such far-reaching changes in the geography of thought and in the apparatus of research, no small nor isolated place belongs to the transformation and expansion of history. That transformation, however, is not yet complete. Its principle is not yet universally or unreservedly acknowledged. It is rejected in many places, or ignored, or unrealised. Old envelopes still hang tenaciously round the renovated figure, and students of history are confused, embarrassed, and diverted by her old traditions and associations. It has not yet become superfluous to insist that history is a science, no less and no more.... History has really been enthroned and ensphered among the sciences; but the particular nature of her influence, her time-honoured association with literature, and other circumstances, have acted as a sort of vague cloud, half concealing from men's eyes her new position in the heavens....

All truths (to modify a saying of Plato) require the most exact methods; and closely connected with the introduction of a new method was the elevation of the standard of truth. The idea of a scrupulously exact conformity to facts was fixed, refined, and canonised; and the critical method was one of the means to secure it. There was indeed no historian since the beginning of things who did not profess that his sole aim was to present to his readers untainted and unpainted truth. But the axiom was loosely understood and interpreted, and the notion of truth was elastic. It might be difficult to assign to Puritanism and Rationalism and other causes their respective parts in crystallising that strict discrimination of the true and the false which is now so familiar to us that we can hardly understand insensibility to the distinction. It would be a most fruitful investigation to trace from the earliest ages the history of public opinion in regard to the meaning of falsehood and the obligation of veracity. About twenty years ago a German made a contribution to the subject by examining the evidence for the twelfth, thirteenth, and fourteenth centuries, and he showed how different were the views which men held then as to truth-telling and lying from those which are held today. Moreover, so long as history was regarded as an art, the sanctions of truth and accuracy could not be severe. The historians of ancient Rome display what historiography can become when it is associated with rhetoric. Though we may point to individual writers who had a high ideal of accuracy at various ages, it was not till the scientific period began that laxity in representing facts came to be branded as criminal....

A right notion of the bearing of history on affairs, both for the statesman and for the citizen, could not be formed or formulated until men had grasped the idea of human development. This is the great transforming conception, which enables history to define her scope.... At the same time, it has brought history into line with other sciences, and, potentially at least, has delivered her from the political and ethical encumbrances which continued to impede her after the introduction of scientific methods. For notwithstanding those new engines of research, she remained much less, and much

24

more, than a science in Germany, as is illustrated by the very existence of all those bewildering currents and cross-currents, tendencies and counter-tendencies, those various schools of doctrine, in which Lord Acton was so deeply skilled. The famous saying of Ranke—"*Ich will nur sagen wie es eigentlich gewesen ist*"—was widely applauded, but it was little accepted in the sense of a warning against transgressing the province of facts; it is a text which must still be preached, and when it has been fully taken to heart, though there be many schools of political philosophy, there will no longer be divers schools of history....

The principle of continuity and the higher principle of development lead to the practical consequence that it is of vital importance for citizens to have a true knowledge of the past and to see it in a dry light, in order that their influence on the present and future may be exerted in right directions. For, as a matter of fact, the attitude of men to the past has at all times been a factor in forming their political opinions and determining the course of events. It would be an instructive task to isolate this influence and trace it from its most rudimentary form in primitive times, when the actions of tribes were stimulated by historical memories, through later ages in which policies were dictated or confirmed by historical judgments and conceptions. But the clear realisation of the fact that our conception of the past is itself a distinct factor in guiding and moulding our evolution, and must become a factor of greater and increasing potency, marks a new stage in the growth of the human mind. And it supplies us with the true theory of the practical importance of history.

It seems inevitable that, as this truth is more fully and widely though slowly realised, the place which history occupies in national education will grow larger and larger. It is therefore of supreme moment that the history which is taught should be true; and that can be attained only through the discovery, collection, classification, and interpretation of facts through scientific research....

History ceases to be scientific, and passes from the objective to the subjective point of view, if she does not distribute her attention, so far as the sources allow, to all periods of history. It cannot perhaps be too often reiterated that a University, in the exercise and administration of learning, has always to consider that more comprehensive and general utility which consists in the training of men to contemplate life and the world from the highest, that is, the scientifically truest point of view, in the justest perspective that can be attained. If one were asked to define in a word the end of higher education, I do not know whether one could find a much better definition than this: the training of the mind to look at experience objectively, without immediate relation to one's own time and place. And so, if we recognize the relative importance of the modern period for our own contemporary needs, we must hold that the best preparation for interpreting it truly, for investigating its movements, for deducing its practical lessons, is to be brought up in a school where its place is estimated in scales in which the weight of contemporary interest is not thrown.

Beyond its value as a limiting controlling conception, the idea of the future development of man has also a positive importance. It furnishes in fact the justification of much of the laborious historical work that has been done and is being done today. . . . The labour is performed for posterity—for remote posterity; and when, with intelligible scepticism, someone asks the use of the accumulation of statistics, the publication of trivial records, the labour expended on minute criticism, the true answer is: "That is not so much our business as the business of future generations. We are heaping up material and arranging it, according to the best methods we know; if we draw what conclusions we can for the satisfaction of our own generation, we never forget that our work is to be used by future ages. It is intended for those who follow us rather than for ourselves, and much less for our grandchildren than for generations very remote." For a long time to come one of the chief services that research can perform is to help to build, firm and solid, some of the countless stairs by which men of distant ages may mount to a height unattainable by us and have a vision of history which we cannot win, standing on our lower slope. . . .

The humblest student of history may feel assured that he is not working only for his own time; he may feel that he has an interest to consult and a cause to advance beyond the interest and cause of his own age. And this does not apply only to those who are engaged in research. It applies also to those who are studying history without any intention of adding to knowledge. Every individual who is deeply impressed with the fact that man's grasp of his past development helps to determine his future development, and who studies history as a science, not as a branch of literature, will contribute to form a national conscience that true history is of supreme importance, that the only way to true history lies through scientific research, and that in promoting and prosecuting such research we are not indulging in a luxury but doing a thoroughly practical work and performing a great duty to posterity.

I may conclude by repeating that . . . if, year by year, history is to become a more and more powerful force for stripping the bandages of error from the eyes of men, for shaping public opinion and advancing the cause of intellectual and political liberty, she will best prepare her disciples for the performance of that task, not by considering the immediate utility of next week or next year or next century, not by accommodating her ideal or limiting her range, but by remembering always that, though she may supply material for literary art or philosophical speculation, she is herself simply a science, no less and no more.

CARL L. BECKER (1873–1945), an influential teacher and scholar in both American and European history, was a prominent critic of the notion of objectivity. The title of his most famous article on the nature of history, "Everyman His Own Historian," gives some clue to Becker's belief that every observer of the past will interpret it from his own viewpoint. In the following essay, which Becker expressly designed to stir discussion, he challenged those who saw historical writing as a simple amassing of "the facts." Consider carefully the meaning of Becker's suggestion that historical facts are really symbolic representations, reflecting the present as well as the past. Does this mean that he derides thorough scholarship or that he believes historians may twist the evidence as they see fit?

What Are Historical Facts?

History is a venerable branch of knowledge, and the writing of history is an art of long standing. Everyone knows what history is, that is, everyone is familiar with the word, and has a confident notion of what it means. In general, history has to do with the thought and action of men and women who lived in past times. Everyone knows what the past is too. We all have a comforting sense that it lies behind us, like a stretch of uneven country we have crossed; and it is often difficult to avoid the notion that one could easily, by turning round, walk back into this country of the past. That, at all events, is what we commonly think of the historian as doing: he works in the past, he explores the past in order to find out what men did and thought in the past. His business is to discover and set forth the "facts" of history.

When anyone says "facts" we are all there. The word gives

From a manuscript in the Cornell University Archives; first printed in *Western Political Quarterly*, VII (1955), 327–40. Reprinted by permission of Cornell University and *Western Political Quarterly*.

us a sense of stability. We know where we are when, as we say, we "get down to the facts"—as, for example, we know where we are when we get down to the facts of the structure of the atom, or the incredible movement of the electron as it jumps from one orbit to another. It is the same with history. Historians feel safe when dealing with the facts. We talk much about the "hard facts" and the "cold facts," about "not being able to get around the facts," and about the necessity of basing our narrative on a "solid foundation of fact." By virtue of talking in this way, the facts of history come in the end to seem something solid, something substantial like physical matter (I mean matter in the common sense, not matter defined as "a series of events in the ether"), something possessing definite shape, and clear persistent outline—like bricks or scantlings; so that we can easily picture the historian as he stumbles about in the past, stubbing his toe on the hard facts if he doesn't watch out. That is his affair of course, a danger he runs; for his business is to dig out the facts and pile them up for someone to use. Perhaps he may use them himself; but at all events he must arrange them conveniently so that someone—perhaps the sociologist or the economist—may easily carry them away for use in some structural enterprise. . . .

What is the historical fact? Let us take a simple fact, as simple as the historian often deals with, viz.: "In the year 49 B.C. Caesar crossed the Rubicon." A familiar fact this is, known to all, and obviously of some importance since it is mentioned in every history of the great Caesar. But is this fact as simple as it sounds? Has it the clear, persistent outline which we commonly attribute to simple historical facts? When we say that Caesar crossed the Rubicon we do not of course mean that Caesar crossed it alone, but with his army. The Rubicon is a small river, and I don't know how long it took Caesar's army to cross it; but the crossing must surely have been accompanied by many acts and many words and many thoughts of many men. That is to say, a thousand and one lesser "facts" went to make up the one simple fact that Caesar crossed the Rubicon; and if we had someone, say James Joyce, to know and relate all these facts, it would no doubt require a book of 794 pages to present this one fact that Caesar crossed the Rubicon. Thus the simple fact turns out to be not a simple fact at all. It is the statement that is simple—a simple generalization of a thousand and one facts.

Well, anyhow Caesar crossed the Rubicon. But what of it? Many other people at other times crossed the Rubicon. Why charge it up to Caesar? Why for two thousand years has the world treasured this simple fact that in the year 49 B.C. Caesar crossed the Rubicon? What of it indeed? If I, as historian, have nothing to give you but this fact taken by itself with its clear outline, with no fringes or strings tied to it, I should have to say, if I were an honest man, why nothing of it, nothing at all. It may be a fact but it is nothing to us. The truth is, of course, that this simple fact *has* strings tied to it, and that is why it has been treasured for two thousand years. It is tied by these strings to innumerable other facts, so that it can't mean anything except by losing its clear outline. It can't mean anything except as it is absorbed into the complex web of circumstances which brought it into being. This complex web of circumstances was the series of events growing out of the relation of Caesar to Pompey, and the Roman Senate, and the Roman Republic, and all the people who had something to do with these. Caesar had been ordered by the Roman Senate to resign his command of the army in Gaul. He decided to disobey the Roman Senate. Instead of resigning his command, he marched on Rome, gained the mastery of the Republic, and at last, as we are told, bestrode the narrow world like a colossus. Well, the Rubicon happened to be the boundary between Gaul and Italy, so that by the act of crossing the Rubicon with his army Caesar's treason became an accomplished fact and the subsequent great events followed in due course. Apart from these great events and complicated relations, the crossing of the Rubicon means nothing, is not an historical fact properly speaking at all. In itself it is nothing for us; it becomes something for us, not in itself, but as a symbol of something else, a symbol standing for a long series of events which have to do with the most intangible and immaterial realities, viz.: the relation between Caesar and the millions of people of the Roman world.

Thus the simple historical fact turns out to be not a hard, cold something with clear outline, and measurable pressure, like a brick. It is so far as we can know it, only a *symbol*, a simple statement which is a generalization of a thousand and one simpler facts which we do not for the moment care to use, and this generalization itself we cannot use apart from the wider facts and generalizations which it symbolizes. And generally speaking, the more simple an historical fact is, the more clear and definite and provable it is, the less use it is to us, in and for itself.

Less simple facts illustrate all this equally well, even better perhaps. For example, the fact that "Indulgences were sold in Germany in 1517." This fact can be proved down to the ground. No one doubts it. But taken by itself the fact is nothing, means nothing. It also is a generalization of a thousand and one facts, a thousand and one actions of innumerable sellers and buyers of indulgences all over Germany at many different times; and this also acquires significance and meaning only as it is related to other facts and wider generalizations. . . .

What then is the historical fact? Far be it from me to define so illusive and intangible a thing! But provisionally I will say this: the historian may be interested in anything that has to do with the life of man in the past—any act or event, any emotion which men have expressed, any idea, true or false, which they have entertained. Very well, the historian is interested in some event of this sort. Yet he cannot deal directly with this event itself, since the event itself has disappeared. What he can deal with directly is a *statement about the event*. He deals in short not with the event, but with a statement which affirms *the fact that the event occurred*. When we really get down to the hard facts, what the historian is always dealing with is an *affirmation*—an affirmation of the fact that something is true. There is thus a distinction of capital importance to be made: the distinction between the ephemeral event which disappears, and the affirmation about the event which persists. For all practical purposes it is this affirmation about the event that constitutes for us the historical fact. If so the historical fact is not the past event, but a symbol which enables us to recreate it imaginatively. Of a symbol it is hardly worthwhile to say that it is cold or hard. It is dangerous to say even that it is true or false. The safest thing to say about a symbol is that it is more or less appropriate.

This brings me to the second question—Where is the historical fact? I will say at once, however brash it sounds, that the historical fact is in someone's mind or it is nowhere. To illustrate this statement I will take an event familiar to all. "Abraham Lincoln was assassinated in Ford's Theater in Washington on the 14th of April, 1865." That *was* an actual event, occurrence, fact at the moment of happening. But speaking now, in the year 1926, we say it *is* an historical fact. We don't say that it *was* an historical fact, for that would imply that it no longer is one. We say that it *was* an actual event, but *is now* an historical fact. The actual occurrence and the historical fact, however closely connected, are two different things. Very well, if the assassination of Lincoln is an historical fact, where is this fact now? Lincoln is not being assassinated now in Ford's Theater, or anywhere else (except perhaps in propagandist literature!). The actual occurrence, the event, has passed, is gone forever, never to be repeated, never to be again experienced or witnessed by any living person. Yet this is precisely the sort of thing the historian is concerned with—events, acts, thoughts, emotions that have forever vanished as actual occurrences. How can the historian deal with vanished realities? He can deal with them because these vanished realities give place to pale reflections, impalpable images or ideas of themselves, and these pale reflections, and impalpable images which cannot be touched or handled are all that is left of the actual occurrence. These are therefore what the historian deals with. These are his "material." He has to be satisfied with these, for the very good reason that he has nothing else. Well then, where are they— these pale reflections and impalpable images of the actual? Where are these facts? They are, as I said before, in his mind, or in some-body's mind, or they are nowhere.

Ah, but they are in the records, in the sources, I hear someone say. Yes, in a sense, they are in the sources. The historical fact of Lincoln's assassination is in the records—in contemporary news-papers, letters, diaries, etc. In a sense the fact is there, but in what sense? The records are after all only paper, over the surface of which ink has been distributed in certain patterns. And even these patterns were not made by the actual occurrence, the assassination of Lincoln. The patterns are themselves only "histories" of the event, made by someone who had in *his* mind an image or idea of Lincoln's assassination. Of course we, you and I, can, by looking at these inky patterns, form in *our* minds images or ideas more or less like those in the mind of the person who made the patterns. But if there were now no one in the world who could make any meaning out of the patterned records or sources, the fact of Lincoln's assassination would cease to be an historical fact. You might perhaps call it a dead fact; but a fact which is not only dead, but not known ever to have been alive, or even known to be now dead, is surely not much of a fact. At all events, the historical facts lying dead in the records

33

can do nothing good or evil in the world. They become historical facts, capable of doing work, of making a difference, only when someone, you or I, brings them alive in our minds by means of pictures, images, or ideas of the actual occurrence. For this reason I say that the historical fact is in someone's mind, or it is nowhere, because when it is in no one's mind it lies in the records inert, incapable of making a difference in the world.

But perhaps you will say that the assassination of Lincoln has made a difference in the world, and that this difference is now effectively working, even if, for a moment, or an hour or a week, no one in the world has the image of the actual occurrence in mind. Quite obviously so, but why? Quite obviously because after the actual event people remembered it, and because ever since they have continued to remember it, by repeatedly forming images of it in their mind. If the people of the United States had been incapable of enduring memory, for example, like dogs (as I assume; not being a dog I can't be sure) would the assassination of Lincoln be now doing work in the world, making a difference? If everyone had forgotten the occurrence after forty-eight hours, what difference would the occurrence have made, then or since? It is precisely because people have long memories, and have constantly formed images in their minds of the assassination of Lincoln, that the universe contains the historical fact which persists as well as the actual event which does not persist. It is the persisting historical fact, rather than the ephemeral actual event, which makes a difference to us now; and the historical fact makes a difference only because it is, and so far as it is, in human minds.

Now for the third question—When is the historical fact? If you agree with what has been said (which is extremely doubtful) the answer seems simple enough. If the historical fact is present, imaginatively, in someone's mind, then it is now, a part of the present. But the word present is a slippery word, and the thing itself is worse than the word. The present is an indefinable point in time, gone before you can think it; the image or idea which I have now present in mind slips instantly into the past. But images or ideas of past events are often, perhaps always, inseparable from images or ideas of the future. Take an illustration. I awake this morning, and among the things my memory drags in to enlighten or distress me is a vague notion that there was something I needed particularly to remember but cannot—a common experience surely.

34

What is it that I needed to remember I cannot recall; but I can recall that I made a note of it in order to jog my memory. So I consult my little pocket memorandum book—a little Private Record Office which I carry about, filled with historical sources. I take out my memorandum book in order to do a little historical research; and there I find (Vol. I, p. 20) the dead historical fact—"Pay Smith's coal bill today: $1,016." The image of the memorandum book now drops out of mind, and is replaced by another image—an image of what? Why an image, an idea, a picture (call it what you will) made up of three things more or less inseparable. First, the image of myself ordering coal from Smith last summer; second, the image of myself holding the idea in mind that I must pay the bill; third, the image of myself going down to Smith's office at four o'clock to pay it. The image is partly of things done in the past, and partly of things to be done in the future; but it is more or less all one image now present in mind.

Someone may ask, "Are you talking of history or of the ordinary ills of every day that men are heir to?" Well, perhaps Smith's coal bill is only my personal affair, of no concern to anyone else, except Smith to be sure. Take then another example. I am thinking of the Congress of Berlin, and that is without doubt history—the real thing. The historical facts of the Congress of Berlin I bring alive in memory, imaginatively. But I am making an image of the Congress of Berlin for a purpose; and indeed without a purpose no one would take the trouble to bring historical facts to mind. My purpose happens to be to convey this image of the Congress of Berlin to my class in History 42, in Room C, tomorrow afternoon at three o'clock. Now I find that inseparable from this image of the Congress of Berlin, which occurred in the past, are flitting images of myself conveying this image of the Congress of Berlin to my class tomorrow in Room C. I picture myself standing there monotonously talking; I hear the labored sentences painfully issuing forth; I picture the students' faces alert or bored as the case may be; so that images of this future event enter into the imagined picture of the Congress of Berlin, a past event, enter into it; coloring and shaping it too, to the end that the performance may do credit to me, or be intelligible to immature minds, or be compressed within the limits of fifty minutes, or to accomplish some other desired end. Well, this living historical fact, this mixed image of the coal bill or the Congress of Berlin—is it past, present, or future? I cannot say. Perhaps it moves with the velocity of light, and is timeless. At all events it is real history to me, which I hope to make convincing and real to Smith, or to the class in Room C.

I have now asked my three questions, and have made some remarks about them all. I don't know whether these remarks will strike you as quite beside the mark, or as merely obvious, or as novel. If there is any novelty in them, it arises, I think, from our inveterate habit of thinking of the world of history as part of the external world, and of historical facts as actual events. In truth the actual past is gone; and the world of history is an intangible world, re-created imaginatively, and present in our minds. If, as I think, this is true, then there are certain important implications growing out of it; and if you are not already exhausted I should like to touch upon a few of these implications. I will present them "firstly," "secondly," and so on, like the points of a sermon, without any attempt at coordination.

One implication is that by no possibility can the historian present in its entirety any actual event, even the simplest. You may think this a commonplace, and I do too; but still it needs to be often repeated because one of the fondest illusions of nineteenth century historians was that the historian, the "scientific" historian, would do just that: he would "present all the facts and let them speak for themselves." The historian would contribute nothing himself, except the sensitive plate of his mind, upon which the objective facts would register their own unimpeachable meaning. Nietzsche has described the nineteenth-century "objective man" with the acid precision of his inimitable phrases.

> The objective man is in truth a mirror: accustomed to prostration before everything that wants to be known, with such desires only as knowing or "reflecting" imply— he waits until something comes, and then expands himself sensitively, so that even the light footsteps and gliding past of spiritual beings may not be lost on his surface and film. Whatever "personality" he still possesses seems to him ... disturbing; so much has he come to regard himself as the passage and reflection of outside forms and events.... Should one wish love or hatred from him ... he will do what he can, and furnish what he can. But one must not be surprised if it should not be

much. . . . His mirroring and eternally self-polishing soul no longer knows how to affirm, no longer how to deny. . . . He is an instrument . . . but nothing in himself—*presque rien!*

The classical expression of this notion of the historian as instrument is the famous statement attributed to Fustel de Coulanges. Half a century ago the French mind was reacting strongly against the romantic idea that political liberty was brought into Gaul by the primitive Germans; and Fustel was a leader in this reaction. One day he was lecturing to his students on early French institutions, and suddenly they broke into applause. "Gentlemen," said Fustel, "do not applaud. It is not I who speak, but history that speaks through me." And all the time this calm disinterested historian was endeavoring, with concentrated purpose, to prove that the damned Germans had nothing to do with French civilization. That of course was why the students applauded—and why Fustel told them that it was history that was speaking.

Well, for twenty years I have taken it for granted that no one could longer believe so preposterous an idea. But the notion continues to bob up regularly; and only the other day, riding on the train to the meeting of the Historical Association, Mr. A. J. Beveridge, eminent and honored historian, assured me dogmatically (it would be dogmatically) that the historian has nothing to do but "present all the facts and let them speak for themselves." And so I repeat, what I have been teaching for twenty years, that this notion is preposterous; first, because it is impossible to present all the facts; and second, because even if you could present all the facts the miserable things wouldn't say anything, would say just nothing at all.

Let us return to the simple fact: "Lincoln was assassinated in Ford's Theater, in Washington, April 14, 1865." This is not all the facts. It is, if you like, a *representation* of all the facts, and a representation that perhaps satisfies one historian. But another historian, for some reason, is not satisfied. He says: "On April 14, 1865, in Washington, Lincoln, sitting in a private box in Ford's Theater watching a play, was shot by John Wilkes Booth, who then jumped to the stage crying out, '*Sic semper tyrannis!*'" That is a true affirmation about the event also. It represents, if you like, all the facts too. But its form and content (one and the same thing in literary discourse) is different, because it contains more of the facts than the other. Well, the point is that any number of affirmations (an infinite number if the sources were sufficient) could be made about the actual event, all true, all representing the event, but some containing more and some less of the factual aspects of the total event. But by no possibility can the historian make affirmations describing all of the facts—all of the acts, thoughts, emotions of all of the persons who contributed to the actual event in its entirety. One historian will therefore necessarily *choose* certain affirmations about the event, and relate them in a certain way, rejecting other affirmations and other ways of relating them. Another historian will necessarily make a different choice. Why? What is it that leads one historian to make, out of all the possible true affirmations about the given event, certain affirmations and not others? Why, the purpose he has in his mind will determine that. And so the purpose he has in mind will determine the precise meaning which he derives from the event. The event itself, the facts, do not say anything, do not impose any meaning. It is the historian who speaks, who imposes a meaning.

A second implication follows from this. It is that the historian cannot eliminate the personal equation. Of course, no one can; not even, I think, the natural scientist. The universe speaks to us only in response to our purposes; and even the most objective constructions, those, let us say, of the theoretical physicist, are not the sole possible constructions, but only such as are found most convenient for some human need or purpose. Nevertheless, the physicist can eliminate the personal equation to a greater extent, or at least in a different way, than the historian, because he deals, as the historian does not, with an external world directly. The physicist presides at the living event, the historian presides only at the inquest of its remains. If I were alone in the universe and gashed my finger on a sharp rock, I could never be certain that there was anything there but my consciousness of the rock and gashed finger. But if ten other men in precisely the same way gash their fingers on the same sharp rock, we can, by comparing impressions, infer that there is something there besides consciousness. There is an external world there. The physicist can gash his finger on the rock as many times as he likes, and get others to do it, until they are all certain of the facts. He can, as Eddington says, make pointer-readings of the behavior of the physical world as many times as he likes for a given phenomenon, until he and his colleagues are satisfied. When their minds all rest satisfied they have an explanation, what is called the truth. But suppose the physicist had to reach his conclusions from miscellaneous records, made by all sorts of people, of experiments that had been made in the past, each experiment made only once, and none of them capable of being repeated. The external world he would then have to deal with would be the records. That is the case of the historian. The only external world he has to deal with is the records. He can indeed look at the records as often as he likes, and he can get dozens of others to look at them: and some things, some "facts," can in this way be established and agreed upon, as, for example, the fact that the document known as the Declaration of Independence was voted on July 4, 1776. But the meaning and significance of this fact cannot be thus agreed upon, because the series of events in which it has a place cannot be enacted again and again, under varying conditions, in order to see what effect the variations would have. The historian has to judge the significance of the series of events from the one single performance, never to be repeated, and never, since the records are incomplete and imperfect, capable of being fully known or fully affirmed. Thus into the imagined facts and their meaning there enters the personal equation. The history of any event is never precisely the same thing to two different persons; and it is well known that every generation writes the same history in a new way, and puts upon it a new construction.

The reason why this is so—why the same series of vanished events is differently imagined in each succeeding generation—is that our imagined picture of the actual event is always determined by two things: (1) by the actual event itself insofar as we can know something about it; and (2) by our own present purposes, desires, prepossessions, and prejudices, all of which enter into the process of knowing it. The actual event contributes something to the imagined picture; but the mind that holds the imagined picture always contributes something too. This is why there is no more fascinating or illuminating phase of history than historiography—the history of history: the history, that is, of what successive generations have imagined the past to be like. It is impossible to understand the history of certain great events without knowing what the actors in those events themselves thought about history. For example, it helps immensely to understand why the leaders of the American and

French revolutions acted and thought as they did if we know what their idea of classical history was. They desired, to put it simply, to be virtuous republicans, and to act the part. Well, they were able to act the part of virtuous republicans much more effectively because they carried around in their heads an idea, or ideal if you prefer, of Greek republicanism and Roman virtue. But of course their own desire to be virtuous republicans had a great influence in making them think the Greeks and Romans, whom they had been taught to admire by reading the classics in school, were virtuous republicans too. Their image of the present and future and their image of the classical past were inseparable, bound together—were really one and the same thing.

In this way the present influences our idea of the past, and our idea of the past influences the present. We are accustomed to say that "the present is the product of all the past"; and this is what is ordinarily meant by the historian's doctrine of "historical continuity." But it is only a half truth. It is equally true, and no mere paradox, to say that the past (our imagined picture of it) is the product of all the present. We build our conceptions of history partly out of our present needs and purposes. The past is a kind of screen upon which we project our vision of the future; and it is indeed a moving picture, borrowing much of its form and color from our fears and aspirations. . . .

If the student of history cannot eliminate the subjective aspects of his endeavors, he can strive to substitute precise investigation for intuitive judgment. To test some hypotheses, the historian can now employ—along with other techniques—computer analysis of data. Professor **STEPHAN THERNSTROM** (b. 1934) here states the case for more rigorous quantitative inquiries by historians and for the value of the computer in such projects. Does he effectively counter the charge that important historical questions are generally not answerable quantitatively? Does he appear to believe that the computer will make the traditional methods of the historian obsolete? Where would he stand in the argument between Bury and Becker?

The Historian and the Computer

Doubtless it is true, as historians are fond of telling their freshman classes, that the study of the past enriches the mind and liberalizes the spirit, undermining the instinctive parochial prejudices of those who have been exposed to only one culture, one world-view, one way of life. But it does not follow, I fear, that historians as a breed are conspicuously liberal and open-minded in their reception of new methodologies and new research technologies. With respect to the subject of this volume, the potential uses of the modern electronic computer, it can only be said that historians have stood not in the vanguard but in the rearguard.

The resistances to computer research have little to do with the machine itself—intimidating beast though it is. They stem rather from hostility toward the concepts and analytical techniques which the computer seems to impose on the user—theoretical constructs,

Stephan Thernstrom, "The Historian and the Computer," from Edmund A. Bowles, ed., *Computers in Humanistic Research: Readings and Perspectives* (Englewood Cliffs, N.J.: Prentice-Hall, Inc., © 1967). Reprinted with permission of the publisher. Footnotes omitted.

and quantitative techniques borrowed from the other social sciences. The suspicion certain professional historians feel toward such borrowing borders on the pathological, as witness the claim of a very distinguished American historian that "almost all important questions are important precisely because they are not susceptible to quantitative answers." Let me say only that anyone who is not blindly and irrevocably committed to the view that all legitimate history is idiographic rather than nomothetic, an art and not a science, should concede two points: first, that there are a great many historical problems of importance which *demand* the analysis of overtly quantitative data (voting statistics, information on wages and prices, population figures, etc.); and second, that the fabric of even the most conventional historical account is studded with terms which are in some sense *implicitly* quantitative ("representative," "typical," "widespread," "intense," "growing," etc.). It is not always possible to translate these intuitive judgments into explicit claims for which supporting quantitative data can be produced, of course, but it sometimes is, and here is another large area within which the computer and the habit of mind it promotes may yield valuable results. By "substituting an examined generalization for an un-examined one," as W. O. Aydelotte puts it, a quantitative approach checks our natural instinct to remember best the cases which best fit our own prejudices and preconceived hypotheses.

Certainly I would concede that historical evidence which is amenable to quantitative analysis is often scarce or nonexistent. But it has been my experience that such data is far more readily available than is commonly assumed. For instance, in my own field of specialization, American urban history, there are rich veins of un-tapped material in manuscript census schedules, election returns, local tax and school records, city directories, and similar sources. Often this evidence is of low quality because of the primitive process by which it was gathered and recorded, but this is hardly an objection to quantitative analysis itself. Indeed, the researcher with a sophisticated knowledge of quantitative techniques is much better equipped to use these materials with proper caution than is the conventionally trained historian, who is prone to rely upon his intuitive judgment of what they portend. Another common objection to quantitative historical research is that the availability of data susceptible to quantification exerts an unduly coercive influence upon the scholar, who may forget the large issues and turn his attention to trivial matters about which statistical data happens to be available. There is some force in this argument, I think, as the painfully trivial character of much contemporary sociological research testifies, but I doubt that scholars sympathetic to quantification are any more exposed to trivializing pressures than those working with other types of evidence—diplomatic notes, let us say. Historians very often let the availability of unanalyzed data rather than the existence of a significant problem determine their choice of subject; thus the cult of manuscript sources, thus the presumption of aspiring biographers that anyone who "hasn't been done" and who has left personal papers behind is worthy of study by virtue of that fact alone.

Perhaps more convincing than any of these general arguments about the value of quantitative historical research, however, is the simple fact that this approach has already yielded significant new findings. Quantitative research in the field of economic history is superabundant, so much so that some of its practitioners have adopted a new disciplinary label, calling themselves *cliometricians.* Their work has already proven of such value that I think we can forgive them that grating neologism. It should be noted in a discussion of the historian and the computer, however, that quantitative research in economic history has tended by and large to be done by men trained by, and holding appointments in, departments of economics rather than history, though recent studies by Bernard and Lotte Bailyn and Theodore Rabb point to a growing interest within history departments as well. The field of political history is humming with activity, and much more can be expected as the resources of the Inter-University Consortium for Political Research become more widely available to scholars. Some of the interesting possibilities here are suggested by Benson's reinterpretation of Jacksonian Democracy on the basis of an investigation into the voting behavior of the New York state electorate, and by Aronson's statistical demolition of the myth of the Jacksonian spoils system. The social characteristics and political activity of elite groups have been illuminated in recently published or forthcoming studies of the French Parliament in the first half of the Nineteenth Century, the English House of Commons in the 1840's, the Reconstruction Congresses, and reformers of the Progressive era. Charles Tilly, who made a major contribution to our understanding of the French Revolution in his investigation of social change and political upheaval in the Vendée, has most recently given us a tantalizing beginning toward a system for classifying and measuring violent political disturbances, and is employing that system in his quantitative study of urbanization and political upheaval in France since 1830.

A specimen the social historian will find of much interest is Merle Curti's computer analysis of social mobility patterns in a Wisconsin frontier community in the 1850–1880 period, though he may remain highly skeptical of Curti's belief that he has provided powerful objective support for Turner's frontier theory—a useful reminder, perhaps, that neither the raw statistical data nor the computer will speak for themselves; that the task of interpreting statistical results is as difficult and fraught with error as other tasks of historical interpretation. Indeed, it is more difficult in one way, for the precision of quantitative data tends to foreclose the common procedure of making sense out of a mass of materials by offering an intuitive generalization which best fits one's own interpretative predilections. Probably this is the reason that quantitative historical studies have more often been effective in dissolving and destroying older categories and hypotheses than in suggesting equally powerful and persuasive new ones. I cannot believe that this is an inescapable problem, and that the scholarly world is destined to remain forever divided between those who offer grand interpretative structures reared on shaky, intuitive foundations and those computer-equipped termites who undermine these grand structures without offering new ones to replace them. . . .

That the computer, properly used, can be of enormous utility to the historian dealing with voting records, economic statistics, or the social characteristics of groups of men should be clear. There can be greater argument, however, over the value of computer analyses of materials of a different kind—words, sentences, paragraphs. One ingenious use of the computer to attack a historical problem—Mosteller's count of the frequency distribution of such minor words as *by, from, to,* and *upon* to infer the authorship of the disputed Federalist papers—seems quite persuasive, but authorship problems are a small and special class, and I don't see that the methodology of the study can be easily extended to other issues.

The technique known as content analysis has much wider application. By breaking down the contents of a document into units which are first labeled by a human coder or by the computer itself with the aid of a dictionary programmed into it, and then mechanically tabulating these units, content analysis purports to provide a more objective, systematic, and sensitive rendering of meaning. There are genuine advantages to this procedure, especially when one is asking rather simple questions of otherwise unmanageably large bodies of material, but the results it yields can be no more sensitive than the coding rules or dictionary employed. I would suggest that in such a field as intellectual history there exist ideas and relationships which cannot be reduced to rules which a machine can follow. One thinks, for instance, of Perry Miller responding to a sermon by Jonathan Edwards. Doubtless a computer, at least if its dictionary were prepared by someone who knew as much about Puritanism as Professor Miller, could pick out certain things in a text that a Miller unassisted would miss, even things of consequence in rare instances. But the converse is equally true, I suspect. I fail to see how a computer could be given a set of formal rules which would equip it to identify some of the most important and yet most subtle connections in a document of this kind—connections which are often ones of delicate emotional shadings, connections which are poetic rather than prosaic.

This is not to dismiss content analysis as a tool for the historian; Richard Merritt's recent study of symbols of American national awareness in colonial newspapers between 1735 and 1775 is one demonstration of its value in treating a certain class of problems, and there are others. Some of the work currently being done by Professor Pool at MIT and by a Stanford University team on communications and decision-making on the eve of World War I may some day influence historical interpretation of that event. At present, however, this research (being carried out, it should be said, by political scientists rather than historians) has been aimed at testing largely psychological propositions of such simplicity and such universality as to be of little interest to the practicing historian: "People pay more attention to news that deals with them." "The higher the stress in a crisis situation, the greater the tendency to rely upon extraordinary or improvised channels of communication." The problem is not that these propositions are self-evident, commonsense truths and thus unworthy of testing. This common complaint against social science research is usually unfounded, partly because it ignores the fundamental principle that for each and every cliché there tends to be an equal and opposite cliché, partly for reasons too complex to go into here. What bothers me is that generalizations of such cosmic sweep, presumably true (or at least interestingly false) of all times and all places, invariably seem arid and empty. While I urge that historians attempt to translate their intuitive generalizations into explicit generalizations, the generalizations I have in mind are less abstract, less sweeping, and more powerful; they are to some degree relative to the context to which they refer, applying to such entities as "American farmers in the Twentieth Century" or even "middle class residents of large American cities in the period since World War II," and might be considered the counterpart in history to what a leading sociologist calls "theories of the middle range." The social scientist will naturally seek to extend the range of these intermediate generalizations and to test their limits, but long before the initial generalization is converted into a proposition of sufficient abstractness to apply universally, the historian will have lost interest in it and have gone back to his business of dealing with events and processes in a limited context. To the extent, therefore, that content analysis is conducted by scholars dedicated to testing universalist models of human behavior, it is unlikely to influence the mainstream of historical writing.

Let me now turn briefly to a narrower subject on which I can speak with greater expertise, my current research on the social history of modern Boston. This study grew out of my belief that the existing literature in the field of social history dealt inadequately with social structure and basic social processes. Even the best work in the field, I felt, depended excessively on evidence which was removed from the daily lives of individuals. My Newburyport study offered several examples which supported the premise from which I began: that some important historical processes could not be understood without microscopic study of individual human actors.

There are grave limitations, however, to the usual microscopic historical study. Biographers can overlook these limitations by persuading themselves (or deluding themselves) that their subjects are intrinsically important. But the social historian who seeks to treat the lives of common men rather than very uncommon men cannot evade the problem of giving general meaning to his findings. The easiest tactic is to describe one's microscopic examination of an obscure group or neighborhood or community as a "case study," a useful phrase which lends an attractive aura of generality to one's painstaking study of the social origins of Armenian grocers in

Boston's North End. But *of what* is this hypothetical investigation a case study? May we generalize from the Armenians to the Greeks, and from them to the Italians and Jews? What does a study set in the North End tell us about the South End, the West End and other neighborhoods of that sprawling complex, Greater Boston? Historians and sociologists alike have been reluctant to consider such questions. Thus William F. Whyte's classic field report on youth in the North End, *Street Corner Society,* leaves us in the dark as to how much of what the author describes reflects basic patterns of working class life in American cities, and how much is due to the particular ethnic group (Italians), the particular neighborhood (the North End), or the particular historical period (the late 30's) Whyte dealt with. Nor does Herbert Gans's interesting recent work, *The Urban Villagers,* which treats working-class Italo-Americans in the West End in the late 50's, go very far beyond *Street Corner Society* in this respect. Ideally, historical studies of the city should employ microscopic techniques for the depth and richness of detail they alone can provide, but should employ them on a sufficiently spacious canvas—spacious temporally as well as physically—to confront the problems that the label "case study" customarily obscures.

It is here, of course, that the development of the electronic computer affords the social historian a great opportunity, for only through mechanical means can the historian master the vast body of materials that he must consult to do a study of this kind. The sources for a comprehensive grassroots social history of the sort I describe are readily available—manuscript census schedules, city directories, local tax records, school records, etc.—and they have occasionally been utilized by historians. But for the student who must collect and analyze it without the aid of electronic devices, the limits imposed by the sheer bulk of this material (and by the tedium it inspires) are very narrow. My own little study of the social mobility of unskilled laborers in Newburyport, which was done without machines, probably involved about as much complexity and drudgery as the ordinary historian can stand, and that study dealt with something less than 10 percent of the labor force of a city of fewer than 15,000 inhabitants. To trace and analyze the career patterns of several occupational and ethnic groups in a much larger community without mechanical assistance would be an utterly unmanageable task. With the aid of a computer it is possible to draw together, examine, and comprehend the life histories of thousands

47

and thousands of ordinary men and women. The historian's microscope can thus be applied to a large enough population over a broad enough time span to provide a dynamic view of the whole of a complex social organism, including such matters as variations in social mobility opportunities during the course of urban growth and industrial change, ethnic differences in the mobility patterns, the flow of population between districts of the city and into and out of the city itself.

I am now attempting something of this sort, employing a computer to map the demographic and social structure of Boston from 1880 to the present. I am feeding into the computer information about three samples of the population in the community, one drawn from 1880 manuscript schedules of the U.S. Census, one from 1910 marriage license records, and one from 1930 birth certificates. This information deals with a host of social characteristics: occupation, place of residence, age, ethnic and religious affiliations, property holdings, etc. Once the samples were drawn, the subsequent occupations, addresses, and property holdings of these men were recovered from later city directories and tax records, so that for a substantial cross-section of the Boston population I have abbreviated family histories which span several decades. There are several questions I hope to explore with the aid of these data (and the Harvard Computation Center). Are there dramatic signs, as popular belief would lead us to expect, that social mobility opportunities in the community became more constricted during the course of industrialization? Are there dramatic differences between the mobility patterns of different ethnic and religious groups? (Again, there is a flourishing folklore about the characteristics of the Irish, the Italians, the Jews, the Negroes, and others, but remarkably little solid evidence.) What is the relationship between intragenerational and intergenerational mobility (how does a father's mobility influence his son's career prospects?), and how are residential and property mobility connected to occupational mobility? Recent sociological research has focused too narrowly on one simple index of mobility, rates of intergenerational movement between manual and nonmanual occupations. I attempted in my Newburyport study to employ a much broader conception of social mobility, and I hope to test some of the ideas developed there—my discovery, for example, of an inverse relationship between occupational mobility and property mobility for unskilled laborers—with the much larger Boston sample.

A word now about a general problem which faces anyone who attempts a study of this kind—that is, the problem of reducing the chaotic mass of raw data to some categories which make it manageable—of developing, for instance, an occupational classification scheme to reduce the hundreds of specific occupations listed on the census schedules to some general types. Each reduction of this kind, of course, involves a *loss*. To know that a man is a "semiskilled laborer" is less revealing than to know that he is a street-car conductor or an operative in a shoe factory. It is a cruel fact that we give up something every time we use a general social category; obviously we should strive to reduce our raw data to order in a way which gives up as little as possible. The point to stress here is that, contrary to the belief of many (possibly most) historians, in dealing with problems of this kind at least, a computer can tolerate much more complexity than an individual human being, and can thus preserve a degree of concreteness that a historian working without a machine would necessarily sacrifice.

This for two reasons. It is very difficult, as I know from painful experience, for a man to cross-tabulate raw data employing more than a very few categories. If one is computing, for example, differing rates of occupational mobility in seven ethnic groups, it is impossibly tedious to utilize more than a half dozen occupational categories (thus 42 cells), and even more tedious and difficult to consider the influence of other variables at the same time. With the cunning spaciousness of a punched card at one's disposal, however, and a tireless device to sort and count these cards, it is possible to use many more occupational categories and hence to remain much closer to the complex reality that the historian of a handicraft age had to abstract from.

A second reason why the computer permits a more complex and more concrete analysis in investigations of this kind is simply that in any study utilizing sampling techniques, the possibilities for refined analysis are severely restricted by the size of the sample. Even a good-sized sample of the population of a modern city, for example, will contain only a few Italian carpenters, so that to examine differences between literate and illiterate Italian carpenters would be impossible; to test the significance of literacy as an influence on career patterns one would have to lump together all carpenters or all Italians to have enough cases for meaningful analysis. But a machine, of course, can handle many more cases than a man; thus a much larger sample can be gathered, and a more subtle and concrete analysis carried out.

I would end on a note of chastened optimism. I do not believe that the computer will revolutionize historical writing, leaving orthodox historians the victims of technological unemployment. Nor do I believe that the overall quality of historical work with computers in the near future will necessarily be very high. Historians will find it difficult to learn enough about computers to employ them in a sophisticated fashion, and it is not unlikely that some who do succeed in mastering the computer will forget (or never learn in the first place) that technical competence in manipulating statistics cannot make up for ignorance of the social context which produced the statistics. But I remain confident that the remarkable increment the computer provides to our ability to do certain kinds of things to certain kinds of historical material, and the contact it will promote between history and the other social sciences, will prove of net benefit.

Regardless of the techniques he uses, the historian—as noted earlier—must observe the past while living in the present. **J. H. HEXTER** (b. 1910), a specialist in British history during the Tudor and Stuart periods, has sought to face up to this predicament. In the following essay he poses the question, "To what extent is the historian the product of his day?" Note why he acknowledges the great influence of the individual historian's "day," while denying that the "times" in which the scholar lives need exercise comparable influence. Though Professor Hexter criticizes both what he labels the "present-minded" and the "history-minded" schools of historical thought, to which position does he appear more sympathetic?

The Historian and His Day

For a good while now a fairly strenuous contest has been in progress between two opposed schools of historical thought. Accepting a classification proposed by one of the keenest though most courteous of the riders in the lists, the division lies roughly between the "present-minded" and the "history-minded" historians. In the course of time many historians have joined one side or the other in the controversy with the natural consequence that there has been some sense and a good deal of nonsense talked on both sides. In general, for some subtle psychological reason that I am unable to fathom, the kind of scholar who, distrustful of "ideas" and "theories," believes that history is all "facts" has tended to take the side of the "history-minded" historians. For more obvious reasons the chronic "do-gooder," who believes that knowledge justifies itself only by a capacity to solve current problems, lines up with the "present-minded" position.

This peculiar alignment has frequently obscured the issues at

Reprinted with permission from the *Political Science Quarterly*, LXIX (1954), 219–33.

stake. It is easy to expose the feebleness and absurdity of those who want only "facts" and of those who want only current problem-solving; and it is fun, too. Consequently the attacks on both sides have often been directed mainly against these vulnerable positions, and it has sometimes seemed as if the main bodies were too busy assaulting their opponents' camp followers to come to grips with one another. For, of course, there is nothing intrinsic to the history-minded position that precludes "ideas" or "theories" or, if you prefer, generalization. Nor is there anything in present-mindedness that demands an optimism as to the efficacy of history as a panacea for current social ills.

Obviously it is not fair to judge either the history-minded or the present-minded historians by the vagaries of their respective lunatic fringes. Casting off the eccentric on both sides, there remains a real and serious divergence of opinion, as yet apparently irreconcilable, maintained on both sides by scholars whose achievements entitle their views to respectful consideration. The divergence is connected at least ostensibly with a fundamental difference in general outlook between the two parties to the argument. In a sense, the present-minded are realists in the field of history, the history-minded are idealists.

The approach of the latter to the problem is essentially apodictic. They say we *ought* not to intrude our contemporary value systems and preconceptions and notions into our reconstruction of the past. They insist that it is our *duty* as historians to understand the past in its terms, not in our own; and they document their thesis with some undeniably horrible examples of what has happened in the last century to historians who looked at the past with the dubious prepossessions, current in their own day, but since invalidated or replaced by other prepossessions equally dubious. Truly there is nothing quite so passé as the intellectual fashions of yesteryear. We find them at once especially ludicrous and especially disturbing when they are worn by men of high talents. We do not like to see the nineteenth-century present-mindedness of so perceptive a man as J. R. Green transforming the roughneck barons of Runnymede into harbingers of nineteenth-century democracy and nationalism. Our embarrassment is even more acute when the victim of present-mindedness is a great historian. We are unhappy when we watch Bishop Stubbs adding Victorian liberalism to the cargo that the Anglo-Saxons brought with them to England from their North German forests. And as the conviction of sin is brought home to us we are warned, "There but for the grace of history-mindedness go you."

Convinced by the dreadful examples arrayed before us we resolve to eschew the wickedness of modernism and thenceforth hew to our obligation to be history-minded. And then a clear and chilly voice says: "But my dear fellows, you can't be history-minded. It might be nice if you could, or it might not, but in any case it is impossible. So all this pother about the obligation to be history-minded is rather silly. Only a particularly repulsive sort of Deity would bind men to do what in the very nature of things they are unable to do." So an almost medieval emphasis on the *duty* to be history-minded is deflected by a rather Machiavellian observation as to the *facts* of life. Medieval assertions about what statesmen *ought* to do Machiavelli met with assertions about what statesmen—the human animal being what it is—are *sure* to do. History-minded assertions about what historians ought to do are met with present-minded assertions of what—the history-writing animal being what he is—the historian is certain to do. The harsh fact of life is that, willy-nilly, the present-day historian lives not in the past but in the present, and this harsh fact cannot be altered by any pious resolve to be history-minded.

What we say about any historical epoch in some way reflects our experience, and that experience was accumulated not in the fifteenth, in the sixteenth, or in any other century than the twentieth. When we look back on the past, we do so from the present. We are present-minded just as all earlier historians were present-minded in their day because for better or worse we happen to live in our own day. Indeed the very horrid examples cited by the proponents of history-mindedness afford irrefutable evidence that the best of former historians were in their day present-minded, and we can hardly hope to be different. So the best thing for us to do is to recognize that every generation reinterprets the past in terms of the exigencies of its own day. We can then cast aside our futile history-minded yearnings and qualms and deal with the past in terms of our day, only mildly regretting that, like all the words of man, our own words will be writ on water. By this intellectual stratagem the present-minded turn—or seek to turn—the flank of the history-minded.

We must admit, I believe, that some points in the argument

of the present-minded are true beyond dispute. It is certainly true, for example, that all that we think is related to our experience somehow, and that all our experience is of our own day. But though this be true, it is also trivial. It is a plea in avoidance dressed up as an argument. Granting that we can have no experience beyond what we have acquired in the course of our own lives, the question is, does anything in that experience enable us to understand the past in its own terms rather than in terms of the prepossessions of our own day? Banal statements about the origin of our ideas in our own experience do not answer this question; they merely beg it.

In the second place, I think we must admit that in some respects all historians are present-minded, even the most determined proponents of history-mindedness. All historians are indeed engaged in rewriting past history in the light of at least one aspect of present experience, that aspect which has to do with the increments to our positive knowledge that are the fruit of scientific investigation. Consider a single example. Up to a few decades ago the Dark Ages before the twelfth century were considered an era of total regression, technological as well as political, social and cultural. Then Lefebvre de Noëttes described results of certain experiments he had made with animal power. He had reproduced antique harnesses for draft horses. In such harness the pulling power of the horse proved to be less than a quarter of what it is in modern harness. But "modern" harness, involving the use of a rigid horse collar, makes its appearance in Europe in the tenth century. So in the Dark Ages a horse could deliver about four times the tractive force that it could in antiquity. Now I am sure that no historian would suggest that we disregard Lefebvre de Noëttes' experiments in our consideration of medieval agrarian history; a four-fold increase in the efficiency of a very important source of power is something that no economic historian can afford to overlook. Yet when we do apply the results of Lefebvre's experiments to medieval agriculture we are being present-minded in at least two ways. In the first and more simple way we are rewriting the history of the Middle Ages in the light of the present because until the present the particular bit of light that was the work of Lefebvre did not exist. But we must go further. It was not pure accident that such work had not been done in earlier ages. Historians in earlier ages would not have thought of going about the investigation of medieval agriculture as Lefebvre did. In making his historical investigations by the scientific, positivist method of experiment and measurement, Lefebvre was distinctly reflecting the preoccupations of his own age and of no earlier one. Scientific-mindedness in this particular area of study at any rate is present-mindedness.

It seems to me that the proponents of history-mindedness must, and in most cases probably do, concede the validity of this kind of present-mindedness in the writing of history; and if this is all that present-mindedness means, then every historian worth his salt is present-minded. No sane contemporary scientist in his investigations of the physical world would disregard nineteenth-century advances in field theory, and no sane historian in his work would rule out of consideration insights achieved in the past century concerning the connection of class conflict with historical occurrences. But this is only to say that all men who are professionally committed to the quest of that elusive entity—the Truth—use all the tracking devices available to them at the time, and in the nature of things cannot use any device before it exists. And of course the adequacy of the historical search at any time is in some degree limited by the adequacy of the tracking devices. In this, too, the historian's situation is no different from that of the scientist. Adequate investigation of optical isomers in organic chemistry, for example, had to wait on the development of the techniques of spectroscopy. If this is what present-mindedness means, then present-mindedness is not just the condition of historical knowledge. For *all* knowledge at any time is obviously limited by the limits of the means of gaining knowledge at that time; and historians are simply in the same boat as all others whose business it is to know.

Now I do not believe that the proponents of present-mindedness mean anything as bland and innocuous as this. On the contrary I am fairly sure they mean that the historian's boat is different from, and a great deal more leaky than, let us say, the physicist's or the geologist's boat. What then is supposed to be the *specific* trouble with the historian's boat? The trouble, as the present-minded see it, can be described fairly simply. The present-minded contend that in writing history no historian can free himself of his total experience and that that experience is inextricably involved not only in the limits of knowledge but also in the passions, prejudices, assumptions and prepossessions, in the events, crises and tensions of his own day. Therefore those passions, prejudices, assumptions, prepossessions, events, crises and tensions of the historian's own day inevitably permeate what he writes about the past. This is the crucial allegation of the present-minded, and if it is wholly correct, the issue must be settled in their favor and the history-minded pack up their apodictic and categorical-imperative baggage and depart in silence. Frequently discussions of this crucial issue have got bogged down because the history-minded keep trying to prove that the historian can counteract the influence of his own day, while the present-minded keep saying that this is utterly impossible. And of course on this question the latter are quite right. A historian has no day but his own, so what is he going to counteract it with? He is in the situation of Archimedes who could find no fulcrum for the lever with which to move the Earth. Clearly if the historian is to be history-minded rather than present-minded he must find the means of being so in his own day, not outside it. And thus at last we come up against the crucial question—what *is* the historian's own day?

As soon as we put the question this way we realize that there is no ideal Historian's Day; there are many days, all different, and each with a particular historian attached to it. Now since in actuality there is no such thing as The Historian's Day, no one can be qualified to say what it actually consists of. Indeed, although I know a good number of individual historians on terms of greater or less intimacy, I would feel ill-qualified to describe with certainty what any of their days are. There is, however, one historian about whose day I can speak with assurance. For I myself am a historian at least in the technical sense of the word; I have possessed for a considerable time the parchment inscribed with the appropriate phrases to indicate that I have served my apprenticeship and am out of my indentures. So I will describe as briefly as I can my own day. I do so out of no appetite for self-revelation or self-expression, but simply because the subject is germane to our inquiry and because it is the one matter on which I happen to be the world's leading authority. Let us then hurry through this dreary journal.

I rise early and have breakfast. While eating, I glance through the morning paper and read the editorial page. I then go to the college that employs me and teach for two to four hours five days a week. Most of the time the subject matter I deal with in class is cobwebbed with age. Three fourths of it dates back from a century and a quarter to three millennia; all of it happened at least thirty years ago. Then comes lunch with a few of my colleagues. Conversation at lunch ranges widely through professional shoptalk, politics, high and ghostly matters like religion, the nature of art or the universe, and the problems of child rearing, and finally academic scuttlebutt. At present there is considerable discussion of the peculiar incongruence between the social importance of the academic and his economic reward. This topic has the merit of revealing the profound like-mindedness, transcending all occasional conflicts, of our little community. From noon to bedtime my day is grimly uniform. There are of course occasional and casual variations—preparation of the ancient material above mentioned for the next day's classes, a ride in the country with the family, a committee meeting at college, a movie, a play, a novel, or a book by some self-anointed Deep Thinker. Still by and large from one in the afternoon to midnight with time out for dinner and domestic matters, I read things written between 1450 and 1650 or books written by historians on the basis of things written between 1450 and 1650. I vary the routine on certain days by writing about what I have read on the other days. On Saturdays and in the summer I start my reading or writing at nine instead of at noon. It is only fair to add that most days I turn on a news broadcast or two at dinnertime, and that I spend an hour or two with the Sunday paper.

Now I am sure that many people will consider so many days so spent to be a frightful waste of precious time; and indeed, as most of the days of most men, it does seem a bit trivial. Be that as it may, it remains one historian's own day. It is his own day in the only sense that phrase can be used without its being pretentious, pompous and meaningless. For a man's own days are not everything that happens in the world while he lives and breathes. As I write, portentous and momentous things are no doubt being done in Peiping, Teheran, Bonn, and Lost Nation, Iowa. But these things are no part of my day; they are outside of my experience, and though one or two of them may faintly impinge on my consciousness tomorrow via the headlines in the morning paper, that is probably as far as they will get. At best they are likely to remain fluttering fragments on the fringe of my experience, not well-ordered parts of it. I must insist emphatically that the history I write is, as the present-minded say, intimately connected with my own day and inextricably linked with my own experience; but I must insist with even stronger emphasis that my day is not someone else's day,

57

or the ideal Day of Contemporary Man; it is just the way I happen to dispose of twenty-four hours. By the same token the experience that is inextricably linked to any history I may happen to write is not the ideal Experience of Twentieth-Century Man in World Chaos, but just the way I happen to put in my time over the series of my days.

Now it may seem immodest or perhaps simply fantastic to take days spent as are mine—days so little attuned to the great harmonies, discords and issues of the present—and hold them up for contemplation. Yet I will dare to suggest that in this historian's own humdrum days there is one peculiarity that merits thought. The peculiarity lies in the curious relation that days so squandered seem to establish between the present and a rather remote sector of the past. I do not pretend that I am wholly unconcerned by the larger public issues and catastrophes of the present. After all I will never be called upon to testify to the purity of my doctrine before the Papal Inquisition of the sixteenth century; but I might be required to do so by less powerfully armed inquests of 1954. Nor am I without opinions on a large number of contemporary issues. On some of them I am vigorously dogmatic as, indeed, are most of the historians I know. Yet my knowledge about such issues, although occasionally fairly extensive, tends to be haphazard, vague, unsystematic and disorderly. And the brute fact of the matter is that even if I had the inclination, I do not have the time to straighten that knowledge out, at least except at the cost of alterations in the ordering of my days that I am not in the least inclined to undertake.

So for a small part of my day I live under a comfortable rule of bland intellectual irresponsibility vis-à-vis the Great Issues of the Contemporary World, a rule that permits me to go off half-cocked with only slight and occasional compunction. But during most of my day—that portion of it that I spend in dealing with the Great and Not-So-Great Issues of the World between 1450 and 1650—I live under an altogether different rule. The commandments of that rule are:

1. Do not go off half cocked.
2. Get the story straight.
3. Keep prejudices about present-day issues out of this area.

The commandments are counsels of perfection, but they are not merely that; they are enforced by sanctions, both external and internal. The serried array of historical trade journals equipped with extensive book review columns provides the most powerful external sanction. The columns are often at the disposal of cantankerous cranks ever ready to expose to obloquy "pamphleteers" who think that Clio is an "easy bought mistress bound to suit her ways to the intellectual appetites of the current customer." On more than one occasion I have been a cantankerous crank. When I write about the period between 1450 and 1650 I am well aware of a desire to give unto others no occasion to do unto me as I have done unto some of them.

The reviewing host seems largely to have lined up with the history-minded. This seems to be a consequence of their training. Whatever the theoretical biases of their individual members, the better departments of graduate study in history do not encourage those undergoing their novitiate to resolve research problems by reference to current ideological conflicts. Consequently most of us have been conditioned to feel that it is not quite proper to characterize John Pym as a liberal, or Thomas More as a socialist, or Niccolò Macchiavelli as a proto-Fascist, and we tend to regard this sort of characterization as at best a risky pedagogic device. Not only the characterization but the thought process that leads to it lies under a psychological ban; and thus to the external sanction of the review columns is added the internal sanction of the still, small voice that keeps saying, "We really shouldn't do it that way."

The austere rule we live under as historians has some curious consequences. In my case one of the consequences is that my knowledge of the period around the sixteenth century in Europe is of a rather different order than my knowledge about current happenings. Those preponderant segments of my own day spent in the discussion, investigation and contemplation of that remote era may not be profitably spent but at least they are spent in an orderly, systematic, purposeful way. The contrast can be pointed up by a few details. I have never read the Social Security Act, but I have read the Elizabethan Poor Law in all its successive versions and, moreover, I have made some study of its application. I have never read the work of a single existentialist but I have read Calvin's *Institutes of the Christian Religion* from cover to cover. I know practically nothing for sure about the relation of the institutions of higher education in America to the social structure, but I know a fair bit about the relation between the two in France, England and the Netherlands in

59

the fifteenth and sixteenth centuries. I have never studied the Economic Reports to the President that would enable me to appraise the state of the American nation in 1950, but I have studied closely Hale's *Discourse of the Commonwealth of England* and derived from it some reasonable coherent notions about the condition of England around 1550. Now the consequence of all this is inevitable. Instead of the passions, prejudices, assumptions and prepossessions, the events, crises and tensions of the present dominating my view of the past, *it is the other way about.* The passions, prejudices, assumptions and prepossessions, the events, crises and tensions of early modern Europe to a very considerable extent lend precision to my rather haphazard notions about the present. I make sense of present-day welfare-state policy by thinking of it in connection with the "commonwealth" policies of Elizabeth. I do the like with respect to the contemporary struggle for power and conflict of ideologies by throwing on them such light as I find in the Catholic-Calvinist struggle of the sixteenth century.

I am frequently made aware of the peculiarities of my perspective when I teach. The days of my students are very different from mine. They have spent little time indeed in contemplating the events of the sixteenth century. So when I tell them that the Christian Humanists, in their optimistic aspiration to reform the world by means of education, were rather like our own progressive educators, I help them understand the Christian Humanists. But my teaching strategy moves in the opposite direction from my own intellectual experience. The comparison first suggested itself to me as a means for understanding not Christian Humanism but progressive education. There is no need to labor this point. After all, ordinarily the process of thought is from the better known to the worse known, and in some respects I know a good bit more about the sixteenth century than I do about the twentieth. Perhaps there is nothing to be said for this peculiar way of thinking; it may be altogether silly; but in the immediate context I am not obliged to defend it. I present it simply as one of those brute facts of life dear to the heart of the present-minded. It is in fact one way that one historian's day affects his judgment.

In the controversy that provided the starting point of this rambling essay, the essential question is sometimes posed with respect to the relation of the historian to his own *day.* In other instances it is posed with respect to his relation to his own *time.*

Having discovered how idiosyncratic was the day of one historian we may inquire whether his time is also peculiar. The answer is, "Yes, his time *is* a bit odd." And here it is possible to take a welcome leave of the first person singular. For, although my day is peculiar to me, my time, as a historian, is like the time of other historians.

For our purposes the crucial fact about the ordinary time of all men, even of historians in their personal as against their professional capacity, is that in no man's time is he *really* sure what is going to happen next. This is true, obviously, not only of men of the present time but also of all men of all past times. Of course there are large routine areas of existence in which we can make pretty good guesses; and if this were not so, life would be unbearable. Thus, my guess, five evenings a week in term time, that I will be getting up the following morning to teach classes at my place of employment provides me with a useful operating rule; yet it has been wrong occasionally, and will be wrong again. With respect to many matters more important, all is uncertain. Will there be war or peace next year? Will my children turn out well or ill? Will I be alive or dead thirty years hence? three years hence? tomorrow?

The saddest words of tongue or pen may be, "It might have been." The most human are, "If I had only known." But it is precisely characteristic of the historian that he does know. He is really sure what is going to happen next, not in his time as a pilgrim here below, but in his own time as a historian. The public servant Conyers Read, for example, when he worked high in the councils of the Office of Strategic Services did not know what the outcome of the maneuvers he helped plan would be. But for all the years from 1568 during which he painstakingly investigated the career of Francis Walsingham, the eminent Tudor historian Conyers Read knew that the Spanish Armada would come against England and that the diplomatic maneuvers of Mr. Secretary Walsingham would assist in its defeat. Somewhat inaccurately we might say that while man's time ordinarily is oriented to the future, the historian's time is oriented to the past. It might be better to say that while men are ordinarily trying to connect the present with a future that is to be, the historian connects his present with a future that has already been.

The professional historian does not have a monopoly of his peculiar time, or rather, as Carl Becker once put it, every man is on occasion his own historian. But the historian alone lives systematically in the historian's own time. And from what we have been saying it is clear that this time has a unique dimension. Each man in his own time tries to discover the motives and the causes of the actions of those people he has to deal with; and the historian does the like with varying degrees of success. But, as other men do not and cannot, the historian knows something of the results of the acts of those he deals with: this is the unique dimension of the historian's time. If, in saying that the historian cannot escape his own time, the present-minded meant this peculiarly historical time—which they do not—they would be on solid ground. For the circumstances are rare indeed in which the historian has no notion whatever of the outcome of the events with which he is dealing. The very fact that he is a historian and that he has interested himself in a particular set of events fairly assures that at the outset he will have some knowledge of what happened afterward.

This knowledge makes it impossible for the historian to do merely what the history-minded say he should do—consider the past in its own terms, and envisage events as the men who lived through them did. Surely he should try to do that; just as certainly he must do more than that simply because he knows about those events what none of the men contemporary with them knew; he knows what their consequences were. To see the events surrounding the obscure monk Luther as Leo X saw them—as another "monks' quarrel" and a possible danger to the perquisites of the Curia—may help us understand the peculiar inefficacy of Papal policy at the time; but that does not preclude the historian from seeing the same events as the decisive step toward the final breach of the religious unity of Western Civilization. We may be quite sure however that nobody at the time, not even Luther himself, saw those events that way. The historian who resolutely refused to use the insight that his own peculiar time gave him would not be superior to his fellows; he would be merely foolish, betraying a singular failure to grasp what history is. For history is a becoming, an ongoing, and it is to be understood not only in terms of what comes before but also of what comes after.

What conclusions can we draw from our cursory examination of the historian's own time and his own day? What of the necessity, alleged by the present-minded, of rewriting history anew each generation? In some respects the estimate is over-generous, in one respect too niggardly. The necessity will in part be a function of the lapsed time between the events written about and the present. The history of the Treaty of Versailles of 1919 may indeed need to be written over a number of times in the next few generations as its consequences more completely unfold. But this is not true of the Treaty of Madrid of 1527. Its consequences for better or worse pretty well finished their unfolding a good while back. The need for rewriting history is also a function of the increase in actual data on the thing to be written about. Obviously any general estimate of the rate of increase of such data would be meaningless. History also must be rewritten as the relevant and usable knowledge about man, about his ways and his waywardness, increases. Here again there has been a tendency to exaggerate the speed with which that knowledge is increasing. The hosannahs that have greeted many "master ideas" about man during the past fifty years seem more often than not to be a reflection of an urge toward secular salvation in a shaky world rather than a precise estimate of the cognitive value of the ideas in question. Frequently such "master ideas" have turned out to be plain old notions in new fancy dress, or simply wrong. Perhaps the imperative, felt by the present-minded, to rewrite history every generation is less the fruit of a real necessity than of their own attempts to write it always in conformity with the latest intellectual mode. A little less haste might mean a little more speed. For the person engaged in the operation it is all too easy to mistake for progress a process that only involves skipping from recent to current errors.

If, instead of asking how often history *must* or ought to be rewritten, we ask how often it *will* be rewritten, the answer is that it will be rewritten, as it always has been, from day to day. This is so because the rewriting of history is inescapably what each working historian in fact does in his own day. That is precisely how he puts in his time. We seek new data. We reexamine old data to discover in them relations and connections that our honored predecessors may have missed. Onto these data we seek to bring to bear whatever may seem enlightening and relevant out of our own day. And what may be relevant is as wide as the full range of our own daily experience, intellectual, aesthetic, political, social, personal. Some current event may, of course, afford a historian an understanding of what men meant five hundred years ago when they said that a prince must rule through *amour et tremeur,* love and fear.

But then so might his perusal of a socio-psychological investigation into the ambivalence of authority in Papua. So might his reading of Shakespeare's *Richard II*. And so might his relations with his own children.

For each historian brings to the rewriting of history the full range of the remembered experience of his own days, that unique array that he alone possesses and is. For some historians that sector of their experience which impinges on the Great Crises of the Contemporary World sets up the vibrations that attune them to the part of the past that is the object of their professional attention. Some of us, however, vibrate less readily to those crises. We feel our way toward the goals of our historic quest by lines of experience having precious little to do with the Great Crises of the Contemporary World. He would be bold indeed who would insist that all historians should follow one and the same line of experience in their quest, or who would venture to say what this single line is that all should follow. He would not only be bold; he would almost certainly be wrong. History thrives in measure as the experience of each historian differs from that of his fellows. It is indeed the wide and varied range of experience covered by all the days of all historians that makes the rewriting of history—not in each generation but for each historian—at once necessary and inevitable.

One of the most widely read—and controversial—historians of our time is **ARTHUR SCHLESINGER, JR.** (b. 1917), who besides writing history has sought to influence it by serving as an adviser to political figures, including President John F. Kennedy, and by speaking out on significant public issues. Schlesinger's career as historian and activist inevitably presents the question of whether the latter role interferes with the former. What pitfalls exist for the scholar who thus combines careers? What benefits, according to Schlesinger, can the historian derive from serving as a participant in history-making?

The Historian and History

The word "historian" is a relatively unambiguous word. It means simply a man who tries to write history. But the word "history" is thoroughly ambiguous. It may refer to events which have taken place in the past; or it may refer to the written record of those events. The historian therefore has a double relationship—to the actual experience, and to the subsequent record of the experience. The problem to which I address myself here is the interaction between history, in both senses, and the historian.

Let us look first at the unambiguous factor in the equation. In our time, the historian tends to be a professional. He is a man trained in his craft, a product of methodical discipline, a member of a guild. His is a quasi-priestly vocation, supposed to liberate him from the passions of his day, to assure him a serenity of perspective and to consecrate him to the historian's classical ideal of objectivity. His creed has been well stated by Walter Lippmann, who once observed that no crisis in human affairs was unique or ultimate:

From *Foreign Affairs,* XLI (April 1963), 491–97. Copyright by the Council on Foreign Relations, Inc., New York, N.Y. Reprinted with permission of the author and publisher.

The world will go on somehow, and more crises will follow. It will go on best, however, if among us there are men who have stood apart, who refused to be anxious or too much concerned, who were cool and inquiring and had their eyes on a longer past and a longer future. By their example they can remind us that the passing moment is only a moment; by their loyalty they will have cherished those things which only the disinterested mind can use.

The phrase "the disinterested mind" suggests the essence of the professional historian's vows. His commitment is to history-as-record, not to history-as-experience, to writing history rather than making it.

It should be noted that this professionalization of the historical craft—this isolation from actual events—is a recent development. In earlier times, there was by no means so rigorous a bar against the chronicler's being also a participant. "The captain of Hampshire Grenadiers," wrote Gibbon, "was not useless to the historian of the Roman Empire." Indeed, until the last half of the nineteenth century, the great historians were, in one way or another, captains of Hampshire Grenadiers. Macaulay, Bancroft, Guizot, Carlyle, Parkman, Henry Adams—all were men for whom the history they wrote was a derivation from the experiences they enjoyed or endured. Latterly we have come to fear that such experience is incompatible with the ideal of "the disinterested mind." This question seems to be worth reexamination.

Historians ought always to make their presuppositions as explicit as possible; and I am bound therefore to declare my own interest. I write as one who, after many years of writing history, has recently had the opportunity to watch history in the making. I have often asked myself whether this experience is likely to strengthen or to corrupt one's purpose as an historian—whether exposure to history-as-experience will improve one's ability to produce history-as-record, or whether it will sever one irrevocably from the ideal of "the disinterested mind." I am by no means sure of the answer to this question—and would only submit now some tentative observations.

The dangers of involvement are self-evident. To act is, in many cases, to give hostages—to parties, to policies, to persons. Participation spins a web of commitments which may imprison the chronicler in invisible fetters. Macaulay was forever a Whig, Bancroft a Jacksonian, Adams an Adams; and their histories became the servant of their loyalties. It is only a partial answer to say that the historian is thus imprisoned in any case; that visible commitment serves at least to alert the reader, while the ostensibly uncommitted historian is left free to shoot from ambush. For the process of involvement does tend to systematize what might otherwise be only vague and fitful inclinations.

Yet involvement has its benefits—and many of these also are self-evident: To take part in public affairs, to smell the dust and sweat of battle, is surely to stimulate and amplify the historical imagination. I have often wondered at those who strive to write about great historical crises like the American Civil War on the assumption that the burning emotions of the day were invalid (though, to be fair to the Civil War revisionists, they condemn mainly the emotions of those who regarded slavery as an evil to be abolished, while cheerfully accepting the validity of the emotions of the slaveholder). Participation in the actuality of history leaves the historian no doubt that mass emotions are realities with which he, no less than the statesman, must deal. Far from being gratuitous and artificial, as the revisionist historians once tried to tell us, the way people feel is an organic part of the stuff of history.

Involvement also increases the historian's knowledge of the operational problems of public policy. The observer who once witnesses the making of decisions under pressure is unlikely ever to write the same disdainful way about the agonizing of Madison in 1812 or Lincoln in 1861 or Wilson in 1917 or Roosevelt in 1941. It is not a particularly difficult trick to say what ought to have been done when you know how the story came out; but, despite E. H. Carr, hindsight is not the safest principle on which to base the writing of history. And involvement not only makes the historian understand a good deal more about the trauma of choice; it also teaches him to distrust a good deal of the evidence on which the historian's reconstruction of that choice is likely to rest.

Nothing in my own recent experience has been more chastening than the attempt to penetrate into the process of decision. I shudder a little when I think how confidently I have analyzed decisions in the ages of Jackson and Roosevelt, traced influences, assigned motives, evaluated roles, allocated responsibilities and, in short, transformed a dishevelled and murky evolution into a tidy and ordered transaction. The sad fact is that, in many cases, the basic evidence for the historian's reconstruction of the really hard cases does not exist—and the evidence that does exist is often incomplete, misleading or erroneous.

Memoranda pro and con cannot necessarily be relied on for an adequate description of the dynamics of decision—or sometimes even for an adequate definition of the genuine issues. Diaries are *ex parte* evidence, designed, consciously or not, to dignify the diarist, and to dish his opponents. Memory is all too often hopelessly treacherous. As for newspaper or magazine accounts, they are sometimes worse than useless when they purport to give the inside history of decisions; their relation to reality is often considerably less than the shadows in Plato's cave. I have too often seen the most conscientious reporters attribute to government officials views the exact opposite of which the officials are advocating within the government to make it possible for me to take the testimony of journalism in such matters seriously again.

For historians of the twentieth century, the problem is compounded by the technological revolution—in particular, by the invention of the typewriter and the telephone. In the good old days, statesmen, quill pen in hand, could write only a limited number of letters. When they had something of significance to communicate, paper was the only means—save face-to-face conversation—of communication. In our time, the typewriter has vastly increased the flow of paper, while the telephone has vastly reduced its importance. Far more documents are produced—and there is far less in them. If a statesman in the twentieth century has something of significance to communicate, if speed and secrecy are of the essence, he will confide his message, not to a letter, but to the telephone. Electronic waves, alas, leave few traces.

But, though the technological revolution complicates the historian's problem of finding out what actually occurred, it does not create that problem. The certitude with which historians are accustomed to pin down the past often results, I suspect, from the convenient fact that there are no survivors to challenge our reconstruction. The historian of the past is, in a sense, little more than the contemporary historian whose witnesses are dead—and who therefore can write without fear of rebuttal. It is not only, as historians like to think, that the passage of time produces more evidence or greater objectivity. It may be too that the passage of time buries those who might otherwise be able to correct or refute the historian out of personal experience.

Sir Walter Raleigh combined as few men have the roles of chronicler and participant; few historians have had to suffer the ultimate criticism of the executioner's ax. I now understand more poignantly than ever before Raleigh's warning in the preface to "The History of the World." The historian, Raleigh suggested, is dedicated to truth; "there is no mistress or guide that hath led her followers and servants into greater miseries." The historian of antiquity, pursuing truth too far off, "loseth her sight, and loseth himself; and he that walks after [truth] at a middle distance, I know not whether I should call that kind of course temper or baseness. . . . [But] whosoever, in writing a modern history, shall follow truth too near the heels, it may haply strike out his teeth."

Only when truth can no longer rise and strike out the historian's teeth is the historian safe—and only then can he remold the past into the desired shape of crystalline lucidity. The passion for tidiness is the historian's occupational disease. Yet the really hard cases tend to be inherently untidy. A case is hard when it confronts men with difficult choices; and choices are difficult when no preconceived solution applies. At such times, those most responsible must of necessity look at the problem from all sides—and often first from one side, then from another. They engage in a collective exercise of thinking aloud, out of which, with luck and leadership, a consensus may emerge. General Marshall used to say that battlefield decisions are taken in conditions of "chronic obscurity"—that is, under undue pressure and on the basis of inadequate information. This is probably the character of most critical decisions in the field of public policy. The historian who comes along later revolts against "chronic obscurity" and tries to tidy everything up. In this way, he often imputes pattern and design to a process which, in its nature, is organic and not mechanical. Historians presumably reject the conspiratorial interpretation of history; but, in a benign way, they often become its unconscious proponents, ascribing to premeditation what belongs to fortuity and to purpose what belongs to chance.

I do not mean to counsel defeatism in this matter. Tendencies can of course be discerned and identified; and a sequence of decisions may supply the evidence for a clear delineation of conflicting programs and policies. But I do doubt whether specific historical episodes can always be reconstructed with the glib exactitude to which historians are sometimes professionally addicted—and I write as one who has sinned more than most.

This recital does not directly answer the question whether involvement in public affairs will corrupt "the disinterested mind." It does perhaps suggest that too rigorous non-involvement may tempt the historian into imposing an excessively rational order on the contingency and obscurity of historical reality. It suggests too that systematic non-involvement may deny the historian clues and insights which could enrich his understanding of the historical process. Involvement may prompt him to ask new questions which open up fertile new possibilities for the profession to explore. I think of Leonard D. White's notable series on the administrative history of the American government as an example—a series produced in answer to a question which had not occurred to several generations of American historians but which did occur to a former member of the Civil Service Commission: How did the thing actually work? And obviously the early economic history of the United States needs to be rewritten in terms of questions arising from our contemporary knowledge of the processes of economic and social development. Historians, in any case, deal more appropriately in questions than in answers. One remembers the dying Gertrude Stein asking her friend, "What is the answer?" and, when she received no reply, saying, "In that case, what is the question?" This should be the historian's creed.

In short, if involvement has its hazards, it also offers its compensations. It may well be more likely than non-involvement to convince the historian of the precariousness of his calling and to bring him to a proper humility before the welter of the past. "The disinterested mind," in any case, is an ideal, not an actuality—and, as the case of Thucydides suggests, it may be more a consequence of temperament than of a preference for the ivory tower over the barricades.

The brush with history-as-experience has therefore given this particular historian a greater skepticism about the feasibility of history-as-record. At the same time, I must add that it has also given me a greater confidence in the utility of the writing of history for the making of history. For there is a two-way relationship between the two forms of history. One must consider not only the impact of history-as-experience on the chronicler but the impact of history-as-record on the participant.

Here my recent experience has given me a strong and unclouded view. I have always been among those who believe that history should be studied for its own sake, not as a guide to the present or a blueprint for the future. I have always questioned the instrumentalist view of history—the notion that knowledge of the past guarantees superior wisdom in making present and future choices. I still am quite sure that the historian is not inherently better qualified than anyone else to offer counsel in the field of public policy. But I have no doubt at all that the significant statesman must have a knowledge of history, an instinct for the grand tendencies, a feeling for the direction in which the world is moving —he must have his own conception of the nature of the historical process. . . .

The conclusion is twofold. If exposure to history-as-experience may lead the historian to doubt a little the precision of history-as-record, it also persuades him that history-as-record forms a basic part of the intellectual climate which shapes the actual unfolding of history in the future—that a sense of history is the indispensable underpinning of statesmanship.

It further persuades this historian that monistic and deterministic visions of history are, except in some broad and trivial sense, wrong—that the sense of history . . . based on the belief in the reality of choice and the plurality of existence, is much more in the grain of the turning world. . . .

In recent years, the most outspoken critics of historical scholarship have not been "relativists" and "objectivists" attacking each other, but a group of young, radical historians protesting against "establishment" history. As the selection below by **STAUGHTON LYND** (b. 1929) indicates, radical historians differ among themselves on the purposes and utility of their work, but for most of them historical study aims essentially at illuminating what human society might be by probing what it has been. Radicals, moreover, see a close connection between their work as historians and their political aim of criticizing and ultimately uprooting the status quo. How does Professor Lynd's conception of historical study differ from Professor Hexter's? Is his definition of "involvement" the same as Professor Schlesinger's?

Historical Past and Existential Present

[P]rofessional historians, whether Marxist or non-Marxist, tend to view history from the sidelines, to give too little weight to that ethical dimension which is critical only for the man who must make decisions, to regard as historically determined what is merely historical past, and, in sum, to do violence to the sense of reality of the historical actor in the present moment. I hope I will not be misunderstood as believing that there are no "historical forces," that historical causation does not exist, that anyone can do anything he wants in history at any time. The point, rather, is that whereas to Marx or Sartre human energy and striving are, as it were, *at the service* of impersonal historical forces, for the man trying to make history such forces are merely matters he must *take into account*

From Theodore Roszak, ed., *The Dissenting Academy* (New York: Pantheon Books, 1968), 101–109. Copyright © 1968 by Random House, Inc. Reprinted with permission of Pantheon Books, a division of Random House, Inc.

in attempting to achieve his self-determined goals. The psychotherapist Viktor Frankl, who himself lived through the concentration camps, reminds us that in that most oppressive of situations men still retained a significant ability to decide what would happen to them. To say the same thing in another way, men can be beasts or brothers at any level of technological development.

How would the work of the historian be different, if man's existential freedom to choose became the historian's point of departure?

The following are some provisional answers.

1. Historians ordinarily assume that history can better be written about events at some distance in the past than about present happenings. No doubt this generalization holds good for certain kinds of events, such as diplomatic events, the sources for which tend to be kept secret until after the passage of many years. But does it apply, for example, to the history of the common man? I think not. Anyone wishing to write the history of the post-World War II civil rights movement could undoubtedly write it better now than five years from now, and better five years from now than a quarter-century hence. The reason is that the "primary sources" for these events are, by and large, neither written nor secret, but are the memories of individual living persons which will become less accurate and accessible as time goes on.

History in the form of chronicling of the present tends to be considered mere journalism, a debasement of what proper history should be, because the passage of time is assumed to give "perspective." Without wholly discounting this argument, it nevertheless seems to me to depend too much on the assumption that there is a single causal pattern underlying events—a skeleton beneath the living tissue—which will appear stark and clear in retrospective view.

The historian's first duty, I believe, is the sensitive chronicling in depth of the important events of his own lifetime.

2. Whether in writing about the recent or the distant past, the historian suggests to the protagonist of the present new alternatives for action. Much as, with or without the help of therapists, all of us occasionally look back to our individual pasts to find strength for new beginnings, so with or without the help of historians Americans who wish to change their present society have used the past as a source for forgotten alternatives. The past serves

us as a means toward that "frequent recurrence to fundamental principles" which the Virginia Bill of Rights advised.

The difference between this use of history and that which follows from a traditional emphasis on causation may be illustrated with reference to the war in Vietnam. The entire American intellectual community has devoted itself, to an extent which must be without precedent, to becoming amateur historians of this conflict. Nevertheless, after all the books and teach-ins the simple question of "Why Vietnam?" remains almost as obscure as in February 1965. An economic explanation of American policy is difficult to demonstrate because American investment in Southeast Asia is relatively slight; but no other coherent hypothesis appears to have been offered. As to the motivation of "the other side," no doubt documents presently unavailable would help somewhat. Yet, to whatever extent Wilfred Burchett is right in his ascription of the origins of the present war to a series of spontaneous local outbreaks in 1957–1959, one suspects that the participants themselves might be hard put to it to provide a definitive causal analysis of the interaction of local grievances, National Liberation Front leadership, and encouragement from Hanoi.

Does this mean that the historian has nothing to offer in Vietnam? or even, in view of the misuse of the Munich analogy by the American government, that a solution might more readily be found if the habit of historical argument could be proscribed? I think not. Where the historian could be helpful, in my opinion, is not by deeper but still inconclusive research into the past, but by projecting alternative scenarios for the future. Considerable experience is available as to the behavior of revolutionary nationalist movements under varying environmental pressures. Without presuming to predict the future, historians might help American policy makers to be more flexible and imaginative by, so to speak, prophesying a variety of outcomes to the present bloodbath. . . .

Thus a second, presently unfamiliar task for the historian would be the projection of alternative futures on the basis of the richness of our past experience.

I can delineate the tasks I am recommending to historians more sharply by exemplifying their opposites. Here again, I draw negative examples from radical historians so as to make it clear that the distinctions I propose are not those whereby radicals have traditionally defined themselves.

Some time ago a student of my acquaintance, a member of Students for a Democratic Society, asked me whether I thought he should do graduate work in history. I said I did not know and suggested that John write to several of the young radical historians. He did so, mentioning in his letter to each that I had told him there were others in the field of American history who were much more optimistic than I about "carving out a radical approach to the field that does not get lost in the usual hair-splitting and inconclusiveness to which the profession is prone."

One of John's answers was from a brilliant young scholar whose particular interest is the history of the inarticulate, as in the work of Albert Soboul, George Rudé, and E. P. Thompson abroad. His letter began:

> I think we know about as much about the role of the common man in American history as we would know about Watts if the McCone Commission were our only source. . . . History has been written by elitists who assumed that when the common man acted he did so for irrational reasons, or because he was manipulated in some way. Much of the excitement of the field to me is that all kinds of good things might have happened that we don't know anything about because of the distortions of history as it has been written.

My own quarrel with this argument is not with its contention that history has been distorted but with its hope that the truth can be restored. Let the reader consider any popular movement of our own day in which he has participated. For instance, take the Mississippi Summer Project of 1964. Half a dozen good books have already been written about it, one a collection of letters by student volunteers, a second narrating in detail a single volunteer's experience, a third in large part composed of documentary appendices. In addition, the event was exhaustively covered by press and television. But do any of us who took part in that adventure seriously imagine that anything more than fragments of it will ever be set down in communicable form? Less than three years after the event, who now knows where the idea for a Freedom Democratic party came from or what really happened at the Democratic party convention at Atlantic City? Considerations such as these regarding

the inevitable inadequacies of contemporary chronicling suggest
skepticism about the possibility of recovering "the history" of popular movements in the past. A few handbills, perhaps some police
records, notices of meetings from contemporary newspapers, the
gossip of upper-class letter writers, very likely fragmentary tax
and election records: is it not scraps like this that we rely on to
reconstruct what happened? And is material like this not infinitely
less adequate than the documentary record that is already so inadequate in the case of more recent movements? I know from experience the temptation to fill in the gaps with personal "wish-
dreams," and to present the result with a spurious air of finality.

John received a second letter from another outstanding young
radical scholar, who said in part:

> I probably disagree with Lynd as to what we can do.
> Politically, neither love nor violence will help us much,
> because we are beyond politics in the sense that this is a
> functionally totalitarian country with a liberal rhetoric,
> and reason and exemplary Christian behavior will not
> alter the politics of those in power. [But] in purely intel-
> lectual terms, radicals have much to do and it seems to
> me that they can define and analyze the nature of the
> beast we confront on a much higher level of sophistica-
> tion and precision than we have up to now.

Is this not quibbling while Rome burns? Can it satisfactorily define
the scholar's task to be able to say "I told you so" amid the ruins?
Should we be content with measuring the dimensions of our prison
instead of chipping, however inadequately, against the bars?

What, then, should be the historian's craft and the idea of
history?

I have made the assumption that what distinguishes the historian from other social scientists is not that he writes about the
past but that he considers things in process of development. "History" and "sociology" are not concerned with different objects;
they are different ways of looking at the same object. Hence the
historian need not be embarrassed if he concerns himself more with
the present and future than with the past.

I have also made the assumption that the historian's business
with the future is not to predict but to envision, to say (as Howard

Zinn has put it) not what *will* be but what *can* be. The past is ransacked, not for its own sake, but as a source of alternative models of what the future might become.

Implicit in my discussion has been a third idea, that "writing history" does not necessarily involve "being a historian": in other words, that chronicling and envisioning are functions which might be as well or better done by many persons in part of their time than on a full-time basis by a professional few. He who *acts* as well as watches may acquire kinds of knowledge unavailable to him who watches only. (That the converse is also true is, of course, a commonplace.)

To these fundamental delimitations of the historian's role I should like to add two major qualifications.

Human beings, at least those born into Judaeo-Christian cultures, appear to need to formulate a collective past. Presumably it will always be mainly the job of the historian to respond to this need responsibly, that is, in a way that does not do violence either to the facts of the past or to the human beings of the present. Despite the alleged antihistoricism of the New Left, the need for a collective past is felt with particular keenness today by young people. Many rebellious young Americans have profoundly mixed feelings when they confront our country's history. On the one hand, they feel shame and distrust toward Founding Fathers who tolerated slavery, exterminated Indians, and in all their proceedings were disturbingly insensitive to values and life styles other than their own. On the other hand, there is a diffuse sense that the rhetoric of the Revolution and the Civil War spoke then and speaks now to hopes widespread among mankind. Thus in November 1965 Carl Oglesby, then president of Students for a Democratic Society, asked an antiwar demonstration gathered at the Washington Monument what Thomas Jefferson or Thomas Paine would say to President Johnson and McGeorge Bundy about the war in Vietnam. And in August 1966, when the House Un-American Activities Committee subpoenaed antiwar activists, the head of the Free University of New York issued a statement invoking the Green Mountain Boys, and the chairman of the Berkeley Vietnam Day Committee appeared in the hearing chamber in the uniform of an officer of George Washington's army.

The professor of history is among other things the custodian of such memories and dreams.

My second qualification is that in a macrocosmic sense I believe Marxism is correct in its understanding of where humanity has been and is going. ... The historian who does not grasp the fact that mankind, whatever else it is doing, is making an agonized transition from societies based on private property to societies which are not, is in my view out of touch with what is happening in the second half of the twentieth century. ...

III.
The Ingredients
of History

INTRODUCTION

It should be evident by now that students of the past view history from vastly different perspectives. Equally important, they focus their attention on a wide variety of matters. Since the historian has as his province the whole of human existence, it would be impossible to catalogue all the ingredients of history. The historian, one scholar has suggested, like Lewis Carroll's walrus, can "talk of many things; of shoes—and ships—and sealing wax—of cabbages—and kings." The readings in this section illustrate but a few of the ingredients, what one of the authors has called the "driving forces in history"—those institutions, social and economic arrangements, men, and ideas that produce historical change.

Historical accounts give prominence to such forces because the scholar, while seeking to recount as accurately as possible *what* happened, must confront the even greater challenge of explaining *why* an episode occurred. In short, as he *describes* the past, he must also strive to *explain* it. Here the student of history must make delicate judgments and assessments. He lacks the chemist's ability to break down a compound into its precise elemental proportions; unlike the physicist, he cannot sum up a reaction in a neat equation. But the historian must nonetheless produce an analysis that will, after a fashion, explain the cause of an event or movement.

A number of influential students of history have offered theories of historical causation that make one type of force dominant in the shaping of civilization. Thomas Carlyle's emphasis on Great Men in history, Karl Marx's on the economic underpinnings of history, Friedrich Hegel's on the role of ideas, and Ellsworth Huntington's

81

on the impact of climate and geography are notable examples of such theories. Most historians, however, do not subscribe to any such overarching philosophy. Indeed, they are likely to be highly skeptical of interpretations that overemphasize one causative agent while neglecting others. But they may, in a particular historical episode, find one ingredient they deem critically important.

The selections below demonstrate the sorts of broad forces that capture the historian's attention. The validity of the particular interpretations is not important at this point, though at a later stage in his work the student may want to give some thought to the specific substantive issues posed. Here the student should simply reflect on the multiple components of history. Gone are the days when history could be described as "past politics." In recent times historians have resourcefully blended politics with economics, demography, social developments, and intellectual currents. As Sidney Hook's essay indicates, students of history have not lost their fascination with the role of leaders. Many, in fact, have borrowed from psychology and psychiatry in their attempts to explain outstanding figures. A few, however, like Jesse Lemisch, have committed themselves to a task requiring even greater ingenuity: infusing the past with a clearer image of the lives and aspirations of the people at the bottom.

The ingredients of history are many, and the best historians neglect none of them. Surely each of the authors included here, whatever his emphasis on a single historical force, would admit that others, too, influenced the times he describes. That makes the historian's task all the harder, for if he tends to shun single-factor explanations, he is charged with weighing numerous elements. Several historians, working on the same period, might assign a particular component varying importance; any historical "problems" booklet demonstrates that. The disagreements sometimes result from an insufficiency or bewildering superabundance of evidence, more often from the individualistic way the historian proceeds to put materials together. Some students of history are attracted mainly to politics, others to economic and social structure, still others to ideas. Some focus their attention on the actions of individuals, others on broad historical forces. If the student is occasionally tempted to bemoan this diversity—which prevents making simple judgments about historical epochs—he should recognize that its effects may well make history more rather than less truthful. No one needs to be told that life is complex. Why should he expect history to be simple?

After nearly a half century of research into a wide variety of topics, the Norwegian historian **HALVDAN KOHT** wrote a book to distill his thoughts on the *Driving Forces in History.* Professor Koht's analysis is eclectic, rejecting any single-track explanation of historical change. But quite clearly, in the excerpts from his book reprinted below, he assigns the state a central role in the shaping of modern history. How, according to Koht's analysis, has the state managed to triumph over those groups and institutions that became its competitors?

POLITICAL INSTITUTIONS:
The Advancing Power of the State

Everyone has observed how institutions created by man's urge to cooperate have themselves become forces in private and social life. Even within man's narrowest circle, the family, children are indelibly stamped by their experiences. Modern psychology has given us deep insights into this early influence on the emotional and intellectual life of the child. When children leave the immediate circle of the home, they are exposed to a multitude of influences from the new society they have thereby joined. They are compelled to learn what they ought to do, and what they ought not to do. Society has its own morality, which inevitably demands more or less uniformity. The individual and society may come into conflict, but even the nature of this conflict is determined by the society within which it occurs. Society irresistibly shapes its individual members according to its own laws. The many are nearly always stronger than the individual. Ibsen's thesis that "the strongest man is he who stands alone" is valid only when he is really alone and has no one else to contend with. The hermit can rule his own kingdom. But in

From Halvdan Koht, *Driving Forces in History,* trans. Einar Haugen (Cambridge, Mass.: The Belknap Press of the Harvard University Press), 137–147. Copyright, 1964, by the President and Fellows of Harvard College. Reprinted with permission of the publishers. Footnotes omitted.

any society, great or small, even the most absolute monarch is shaped by the social forces that encircle him.

I shall take up for special consideration the one of those social institutions that in our day has developed into possibly the strongest force of all. This is the state. It is most instructive to observe how the state has acquired its dominance within the historical period. Indeed, "the historical period" begins with the state. Everything that precedes the state is prehistoric. For this reason it is not strange that the state has come to fill most of the space in textbooks of history. To a great extent they have been written by the state itself. When historians try to find space for other topics in their textbooks, it is part of the struggle *against* the power of the state.

... The state was founded as a military force under the leadership of kings, whose function it was to defend their country when it was at war with other states, or even to subjugate other states under them. Soon the kings had to begin taxing their people in order to maintain the armed forces, besides mobilizing them to make war. Since the kings also were entrusted with the maintenance of domestic peace, they had to strengthen the judicial authority that society had established to provide peace and justice. In the earliest Norwegian laws there was no judicial authority other than the one exerted by the great assemblies called *things*. Yet the very earliest kings from Harald the Fairhaired on were praised by the bards because they punished thieves and robbers. During the following centuries judicial authority was concentrated more and more in the hands of the king and his servants. Power was being centralized in the state. The same thing was happening in other countries also, in one way or another.

As the state gradually drew more and more areas of social life under its dominion, it happened time and again that competitors arose who also wanted power over men. One of the most important of these was organized religion. To be sure, this applies only to Christianity and the Christian church. In classical times state and religion were so intimately joined that they made only a single power together. Religious life was not at any rate organized into a central power that could compete with the state. The codes of law were often held to be of divine origin. This was the case with the Mosaic code among the Jews. The Mohammedan state also issued from a religious movement, and its Koran was as much a secular as a religious code. State and religion remained indissolubly joined in all Moslem countries. For this reason religion became the most important element in the national movements of these countries. It became a Mohammedan nationalism, not Egyptian, or Syrian, or Berber.

Christianity was different. It grew up outside the state and often in conflict with the state. The organized Christian church became a power of its own and helped to lead Europe forward into the new era which we call the Middle Ages.

In calling the church a "competitor" of the state, I am using the word in its original meaning of something that moves together with, or alongside of, and is therefore in cooperative rather than in unfriendly opposition. After Constantine the Great had made Christianity a state religion, the state took over the task of building the Christian church. The state called the great church councils, and the state determined what the true Christian doctrine was going to be. The state gave the church power within its own borders.

This intimate collaboration between secular and religious authority proved to be permanent in that empire which called itself Roman, but which we usually call Byzantine. In western countries the development was different. Charlemagne tried to restore the Roman Empire in the West, and as I have mentioned in another connection, he proclaimed that he would rule his empire according to Christian principles. It proved, however, to be impossible to keep all of western Europe united under the Roman emperor. The result was that in western Europe state and church came to have different limits. The church asserted the unity of all Catholic countries at the same time as these were politically dispersed into many distinct states.

This did not immediately interfere with cooperation between the church and the heads of state. An entirely erroneous view, which often has been expressed in modern historical writing, is that the church was constantly attempting to take over secular authority and push the state aside, or even to become its master. Among Protestant historians, and later among the positivists, one will find the advance of the church described as "aggression" against the state, and an expression of ecclesiastical "arrogance." This is a projection back into an earlier period of experiences and events from those later ages when conflict had arisen between state and church. The Norwegian historian J. E. Sars protested against this kind of anachronistic historical writing as long ago as 1856. I have myself tried in various connections to show that throughout the early Middle Ages state and church lived in complete harmony. I have been able to demonstrate that when kings accepted their countries as a fief from a Christian saint, such as St. Peter, St. Dionysius, or St. Olav, they often did so in order to protect the independence of their country.

Actually, the church was at first only concerned about establishing Christian law and morality in areas with which the state at that time was not concerned, for example, in marriage. Even heathen barbarians had their marital morality, but marriage, the life together of a man and a woman, was not subject to any public law. The church imposed a variety of rules and regulations, such as the requirements of consecration and sexual purity, prohibitions on marriage between close relatives, and severe punishments for all violations of these new laws. Another area was aid to the poor and the infirm. The church succeeded in establishing a tax, the tithe, which was used, among other things, for helping the poor. The church built hospitals for those who fell ill. It was a matter of course that the church had to provide for instruction in Christianity, and even if common schools were not immediately established, there was at least a beginning. Proper schools had to be founded for those who were to be priests; in this way higher education came into being. These activities provided a vast field of operations for the church, a whole array of social activities directed by the clergy. I need only mention such additional fields as church architecture and art. We are here concerned only with the social institution of the church and the power it came to wield.

There were periods when state and church got into conflict, for example over judicial authority. As the church developed a stronger organization, it demanded the right to punish its own servants and to mete out justice, even for ordinary secular crimes. Not all kings were willing to accept this extension of its authority. The church also wished to reduce the power wielded by the state in choosing the bishops of the church. In the eyes of the kings, the worst presumption of the church was its claim to the right of deciding whether a head of state was a tyrant, a rebel against God. It was by this authority that Pope Gregory VII excommunicated Emperor Henry IV, and that Pope Innocent III did the same to King Sverre of Norway.

In this way clashes arose between state and church that involved both principles and power. The relationship between state and church was debated in learned treatises. One of the earliest of these was one that King Sverre caused to be written shortly before the year 1200. This document was rather less theoretical in its approach than many of those that followed it. Intellectual weapons were thus employed in the battle, but they were not the only ones. The church, of course, had no others, while the state could also employ the force of arms and politics. In the end the state won out.

The decision came with those events that we customarily unite under the name of the Reformation. We think here first and foremost of the countries that broke out of the Catholic church and established a creed that made certain changes in Christianity. The program of reformation, however, which demanded that both "head and limbs" of the church should be "reformed," extended far beyond the so-called Reformed countries. To a great extent it was effected in Catholic countries as well, by a drastic reduction of the authority of the church. All along the line, the church was defeated as an institution of power. This defeat was, of course, greatest in those countries where the church was converted into a state church and thereby became an organ of the state. Only one of the reformers, Calvin in Geneva, tried to build up in his state a kind of theocracy, a rule of God, where state and church were one. English Puritans later tried something of the same, in England as well as in America. In either case, the end of it was that the church fell under the domination of the state, or at least lost all of its political functions.

The conflict between church and state was not thereby ended, either in the Protestant or in the Catholic countries. The church was anxious to win back what it had lost. This was one of the primary purposes of the new order of Jesuits. A time was to come when lovers of liberty adopted the cry of Voltaire, "Crush the infamous one!" (*Écrasez l'infame!*) The "infamous one" was nothing else but the church itself.

In most places the conflict arose over the schools. Secular schools had been established during the last centuries of the Middle Ages—universities for advanced education and schools for elementary education in the city-states of northern Italy and the Netherlands. In the modern period the governments of all countries began more and more to organize such secular education at all levels of teaching. The state and the church were often at loggerheads over the mastery of these schools. The bitterest strife broke out in

France in the nineteenth and early twentieth centuries. Again the state carried off the victory, in spite of a variety of compromises.

At the same time as the state took away the power of the church, other innovations developed in its activity. The change was not due to any single factor. In the early Middle Ages the formation of the Christian church and the breakup of the Roman Empire had both characterized the new era. Now there were, in addition to the religious reformation, the new explorations and the tremendous advances in seafaring and commerce. European life was transformed, and the state became a leader in establishing policies of trade and colonial expansion.

The state had not been entirely without economic interests even earlier, but the political leadership had mostly been concerned with the income and the expenses of the state itself. These purely financial considerations did not leave the rulers much time to think about the prosperity of their people. . . .

Only in the small city-states of northern Italy, Germany, and the Netherlands were the governments compelled to think of measures for promoting the native economy. The German cities learned that trade meant power, and they exercised it by using blockades as weapons against foreign governments that would not let them have their way. The Hundred Years' War between England and France in the fourteenth century was largely caused by disagreements over the Dutch wool and cloth trade.

In this way economic questions began to enter politics. It was not until the sixteenth century, however, that they became one of the central concerns of rulers. It quickly became apparent that trade with the new countries in America and East Asia required the backing and protection of the state. Any territory that the state wanted to exploit had to be won by force of arms. This period of colonial expansion led to an entirely new theory of the state, the doctrine of mercantilism. This theory declared that it was a major concern of the state to strengthen the national economy in every possible way. The state became an instrument of the economic interests of its citizens, particularly those who were engaged in trade and in production for export. The middle class seized power in the state and centralized its government more and more for the promotion of economic advancement.

Rapid and extensive centralization characterized the mercantilistic state. As the number of new enterprises expanded, the state felt a need for more and more servants. The state became a state of bureaucrats, who built roads and canals, abolished internal tariff barriers, organized public postal services, and surrounded the country with a network of customs offices. The state established trade concerns and industrial enterprises and often invested great capital sums in these. The concerns were given monopolies as a kind of state institution. Now that the interests of the citizenry came to be paramount, the state began to organize public schools that were built not upon Latin, the book-language of the church, but on the language that was being used in government offices. All the schools were to have a common national language. The unity of the state was the law in all areas, to the detriment of local peculiarities. The fact that the king could say, "I am the state," was due to the fact that he was the hub of its centralization. The actual rulers, however, were the civil officials.

After all this regulation and regimentation came the inevitable reaction. The middle class grew so strong that it wished to manage by itself and to free itself from the dominance of the state. The state had helped to give it strength. Now that it had come of age, it rose against the state and demanded freedom. Liberalism replaced mercantilism. Later on, demands would be raised for national protectionism and other aids to the native economy. This, too, was an expression of economic growth.

I will not pursue this story any further. I merely wish to point out that a multitude of organizations rose up to become new competitors of the state. The world entered into the era of what was long called "associations." These were economic and professional organizations of all kinds—societies of traders and craftsmen, workers and farmers, political parties of all shades, discussion clubs and societies for self-improvement—societies without number for all kinds of interests, material, intellectual, or even physical. Some societies made it their goal to solve certain social problems that the state had not yet taken up, such as the care of particular groups of handicapped people.

In the period when the fashionable cry was for liberty, the liberty of association was one of its demands. The old state did not approve of private organizations that had greater aims than purely social intercourse. It frowned on all organizations that were not regulated by the state itself, as were the craft guilds, for example. These guilds were targets of the liberals, who wanted to substitute their own free associations. The new societies were in principle voluntary, but people could be forced into them because of the power the societies had over certain branches of industry, or certain political parties. They could develop a power that even defied the state, as appeared when they organized strikes, or lockouts, or boycotts.

The policy of the state in this situation could not be one of suppressing such organizations, but rather to try to incorporate them into the state itself. This was the program that socialism developed in various forms. The earliest socialists dreamt about the possibility of escaping both the state and the private economic organizations by building up small independent cooperative societies. This proved to be entirely utopian, as it was usually called. The associations had to find their place within the state.

This has become the task of the twentieth century. The most significant innovation was no doubt the many kinds of social insurance that began to be established in country after country from the 1880s, which have expanded more and more as the years have passed. The state has also given subsidies to many other kinds of social welfare. Such subsidies have inevitably led to state control, which has been established in one area of social life after the other. Everywhere we find an organized cooperation between the government and private organizations, particularly in economic life. . . . The state has assumed a plethora of new duties, one of the most important and successful being the duty to provide work for the entire population. The state has developed from being merely a judicial state to what we now call a welfare state. We ask that it shall employ its power for the promotion of happiness among all people. Even more, the state has become an instrument for new economic enterprise, a true driving force in progress.

If most historians still concentrate mainly on politics, many students of the past have come to recognize that the economic and social structure of an era may be at least as important in shaping events. Without lapsing into narrow economic determinism, the perceptive historian can distinguish socio-economic patterns that had sweeping political consequences. JACQUES GODECHOT (b. 1907), a French scholar who has broadened his attention from the French Revolution to the wider "Atlantic Revolution" of the eighteenth century, here probes those economic and social developments that contributed to revolutionary ferment. Notice that in addition to quite sophisticated analysis of these developments, Godechot explains why the same phenomena did not have identical results in all the Atlantic nations.

ECONOMIC AND SOCIAL FORCES:
Structural Causes of Revolutions

Causes common to a revolutionary movement extending over half of Europe and the European-colonized part of America necessarily lay very deep in the character of society. In the first place, these causes were certainly bound up with transformations in the social structure itself. This was asserted in 1793 by Barnave, a French revolutionary and former member of the Constituent Assembly, who died later that year on the guillotine. In an interesting book, *Introduction to the French Revolution,* which was published for the first time in 1843 and republished in 1960, Barnave showed that everywhere in Europe society had been originally feudal, with the immense majority of inhabitants living under the domination of the landed aristocracy. Possession of the land had been the only source of wealth and the basis of power. The great discoveries of the sixteenth century and the rise of transoceanic navigation led to development of a new social class, the commercial bourgeoisie, and to the growth of great cities, in particular the ports situated on either side of the ocean—London, Paris, Rouen, Antwerp, Amsterdam, Hamburg, New York, and Philadelphia.

The commercial bourgeoisie of these great cities spurred the expansion of industry, which became very rapid after the late eighteenth century thanks to the invention of the steam engine and other machines. The labor force expanded rapidly too. The revolution originated ultimately in the desire of the new classes, especially the bourgeoisie, to come to power. Nor, declared Barnave, was the revolution limited to a single country; it was a "European revolution with France at its apex."

Present-day historians, recognizing the truth of Barnave's ideas, have also been struck by their "Marxist" formulation. They regret, however, that Barnave spoke of a purely "European" revolution, for the revolutionary movement first showed its force across the Atlantic. It would be better to speak either of the "Revolution of the West" or of the "Atlantic Revolution."

If as a whole the pattern described by Barnave is correct, it is nevertheless rather vague. It can now be made more precise as a result of the numerous studies of the social structure of the Western countries made during recent years. Although these studies bring out very noticeable regional differences, they also demonstrate incontestable similarities.

Two types of social structure can be distinguished in Europe and America. In some regions, the peasants were usually owners of the land; in other regions they worked as serfs or slaves upon lands belonging to large landowners, who were generally noblemen. Europe west of the Elbe and North America above the Potomac belonged to the first type of structure. In these countries the tiller of the soil was either its absolute owner, in the Roman sense of the word, or a manorial tenant—actually the owner of the land subject to the payment of manorial dues which varied in importance according to the region. Or he might be a renting farmer, paying either a money rent or a share of the crop. Of course, there were landless peasants, whom the French called *brassiers* because they had only their arms (*bras*) with which to work; but they could move about freely and take up another trade if they wished. Property in land was generally small and scattered. Although the nobility and the

Church still owned an important portion of the land—in some regions as much as 30 to 40 percent of the acreage—it must not be forgotten that a large fraction of the nobles' lands and the greatest part of the clergy's land were rented to peasantry. This was the fundamental agrarian structure of western Germany, the Low Countries, France, northern Italy, and northern Spain. In England small landed property was becoming less important, giving way to great enclosed estates which the landlord farmed with free wage-laborers. In central and southern Italy and in most of Spain large estates or *latifundia* predominated, but the agricultural workers who cultivated them—very badly, it may be added—lived in big villages of urban character and were completely free. Furthermore, the agrarian system presented significant variations. In the west and south of Western Europe, the fields were generally irregular in form and were enclosed by hedges; this system further strengthened the peasant's individualism. In the north, on the contrary, the open-field system prevailed. The parcels of land were grouped into "fields" (*soles*) or "seasons"; everyone who cultivated the same seasonal field was compelled to plant the same crop. Once the harvest was brought in all the inhabitants of the village, including those who possessed no land, were entitled to bring their livestock to graze upon the stubble. This was the system of "stubble right" (*vaine pâture*), to which the *brassiers* were strongly attached. However, the big landowners, noble and bourgeois alike, increasingly sought the abolition of stubble rights so that they could make their fields more productive.

This structure of peasant society in Western Europe forms an extraordinary contrast to the system that prevailed east of the Elbe river. While west of the Elbe serfdom remained exceptional (in France in 1789 there were less than a million serfs—more precisely *mainmortables,* peasants who could not inherit property without paying a fee to their lord), serfdom was the rule beyond the Elbe. The peasant serfs were almost never owners, tenants, renters, or even sharecroppers. They were *adscripti glebae,* bound to the soil and sold with it. The peasants of Eastern Europe, in their immense majority without any education, passively accepted the rule of the lord, who enjoyed very extensive and almost absolute powers over them. The mentality of the Prussian Junker and the Polish or Hungarian magnate was therefore very different from that of the French squire, the British landlord, or even the Neapolitan baron.

South of the Potomac in the British North American colonies, and in the French, Spanish, and Portuguese colonies of Central and South America the land was tilled by black slaves imported from Africa. Conditions resembled those on the estates of Eastern Europe, although the white proprietors would have been indignant to hear themselves compared to Polish or Russian noblemen. They considered slavery a "peculiar institution" bound up with the tropical or equatorial climate; they saw no reason whatever for it to disturb their feeling of belonging to the Western world, which they held to be the vanguard of civilization.

If we pass from the peasantry to an examination of the structure of the other social classes, the contrast between the regions of Eastern and Western Europe becomes even sharper. Everywhere in Western Europe there existed a rich and active bourgeoisie which inhabited numerous large cities. London, Paris, and Naples exceeded 500,000 inhabitants; Hamburg, Liverpool, Amsterdam, Nantes, and Bordeaux attained or passed 100,000 and it would take too much space to list the cities with more than 50,000 inhabitants. East of the Elbe it is possible to cite only Warsaw, Moscow, and St. Petersburg among cities with more than 100,000 population. In Western Europe the bourgeoisie formed a powerful class whose wealth was comparable to, and sometimes even surpassed, that of the nobility. They were in control of almost all trade and the largest part of industry. Furthermore, industry had begun a full-scale revolution in 1750. The invention of the steam engine and various other machines, especially in the textile industry, resulted in the appearance of the first large factories, most of which were in the hands of the bourgeoisie. East of the Elbe, however, the bourgeoisie was extremely small in numbers. Internal trade was almost entirely in the hands of Jews; foreign trade was conducted by the nobility or even by the state.

In Western Europe one of the principal causes of social disturbances consisted in the rise of the bourgeoisie. They possessed wealth and desired power. They did in fact participate in the exercise of power in England, the Netherlands, and several regions of Italy but wanted to gain power in France and to have a larger share of it in Italy, Ireland, and the British colonies of America.

We thus see that the rise and ambitions of the bourgeoisie formed one of the elements of social disorder in the West. But other factors of more acute character resulted from the expansion of the population.

94

Nowadays sociologists agree that quantitative changes of the population structure are among the essential causes of the revolutions of the contemporary world. No one disputes that the acquisition of independence by the countries of North Africa was essentially prompted by an increase in their population at a rate so rapid that some writers have characterized it as "demented." Why should it have been otherwise in the past? More and more numerous studies of the demographic evolution of the West in the eighteenth century show that a considerable increase also occurred then. Of course it was not a new phenomenon: the population of the globe has been growing ever since the origin of mankind. But today we are quite sure that this growth was not continuous but came in spurts. Europe probably did not have many more inhabitants at the end of the seventeenth century than it had at the end of the fifteenth. During the eighteenth century, on the contrary, the population of Europe doubled on the average, although the increase varied according to the region. It was very large in England but less in France. In Venice the population actually became smaller. The figures on population in Poland and Russia are uncertain, but the fact of growth is indisputable. More important perhaps than the increase in numbers as such was the modification of the demographic pattern. Between the fifteenth and the eighteenth centuries the failure of the European population to grow had been the consequence of a series of profound crises, epidemics (generally called "plagues"), and wars. Plagues and wars in particular resulted in catastrophic drops in the population. To be sure, the high birth rate permitted a rapid return to the previous figure, but then new crises followed which prevented any further rise. Infant mortality was considerable. More than half the newborn did not live beyond one year of age. Life expectancy was short; the average life extended little beyond twenty-four years. This whole pattern was transformed during the eighteenth century. Although infant mortality remained very high and decreased only very, very slowly, the adult mortality rate diminished considerably; thus life expectancy increased. In France the total population, which had never exceeded 18 million since the fourteenth century, passed this figure around 1730 and reached 26 million in 1789. The population of the whole of Europe passed from 100 million to about 200 million between 1700 and 1800.

This was a phenomenon of capital importance. The increase of the population created two fundamental problems. One was subsistence: would the augmentation of food production keep up with the growth in the population? The other was employment: would the surplus population be able to find work? These questions preoccupied the scientists and philosophes of the eighteenth century. They gave various and often contradictory replies. The Englishman Thomas Malthus, a pessimist, favored reducing the number of births.

In any case we are in the presence of the fact that the European population doubled. What were the consequences of this increase? Did it cause the disorders and the revolution? So far as expansion of food production is concerned, the problem is very complex. It seems well established at the present time, thanks to recent studies, that the increase in the European population was due first of all to improvement of agricultural production. The discovery of America in the late fifteenth and sixteenth centuries made available to Europeans new plants which either were more nutritious or had a bigger yield than the crops which had long been cultivated in Europe. These included maize (American corn), which had a yield of 32 to 1, while the best varieties of wheat sowed in Europe yielded only three or four to one; the potato, which grew very well in poor soils; tobacco, whose leaf was in great demand and sold at a very high price; and vegetables such as the kidney bean and the pumpkin. These plants were introduced into Europe as early as the sixteenth century but were accepted slowly, and the consequences of their cultivation only became evident in the eighteenth century. There is no doubt that they improved the diet of the European peasant and thereby contributed to increasing his resistance to disease. Hence adult mortality fell. The progress of hygiene and medicine does not seem to have played a major part in reducing mortality. But as the European population increased, the surplus in agricultural products decreased. Other ways for increasing production had to be considered. The English agronomists and the French physiocrats began scientific study of the process of cultivation of the soil. They recommended development of pasturage by means of artificial meadows, abandonment of triennial or biennial rotation of crops (which left as much as half the ground fallow each year), development of industrial crops, selection of seed, and suppression of open pasture by means of the enclosure of farmlands. These suggestions were often adopted. In France, butcher shops increased in number and had spread even to the smallest villages by the end of the eighteenth century. Nonetheless it does seem a fact that agricultural production was unable to keep up with the increase in the population. After 1770, bad crops due to weather conditions (excessive rainfall or heat) resulted in famines such as Western Europe had not seen for fifty years.

Employment was a different problem. When population began to increase, men easily found jobs in agriculture, which was developing rapidly. In certain countries of Western Europe, like France, the Netherlands, Germany and especially England, the start of the Industrial Revolution and the building of big factories resulted in the creation of new jobs. But soon there were not enough jobs, and unemployment developed. The number of jobless vagrants in France on the eve of the revolution was considerable. Here is the significant complaint made by the villagers of La Caune, near Châlons, in their grievance list (*cahier de doléances*) in 1789: "The number of our children makes us despair. We do not have the means to feed or clothe them." An inquiry conducted by the "committee on mendicancy" of the Constituent Assembly in 1790 revealed that in about half of France (44 departments out of 86) the number of the "indigent" (that is, the unemployed) was more than 10 percent; in six departments, including Haute-Garonne, Le Nord, and Pas-de-Calais, it reached one-fifth of the population. In England and Germany the employment situation was less difficult: in the former country big industry was more developed; in the latter overseas emigration was more important. However, despite the great extent of vacant land, the arrival of an increasing number of immigrants in America confronted that country with problems like those which the increase in population placed before Europe.

The considerable increase in the population of the Western world resulting from introduction of new plants of American origin into Europe must be considered incontestably one of the major causes of the revolutions of the Atlantic world. Indeed, it was from the innumerable unemployed that were recruited not the leaders, but the troops, of the revolutionary armies.

The difficulties met after 1770 by a young population in the full flood of expansion are bound up with the economic cycle. The business cycle has not been studied in its entirety for the whole of the West but only in some individual countries—England, Spain, Holland, and especially France. Tables of prices and sometimes of wages have been established and curves drawn. The examination of these curves demonstrates that in a general manner prices rose slowly from about 1730 to 1770. From 1770 to 1790 we observe a plateau marked by very accentuated sawteeth in the curves. These peaks and hollows on the graphs are the indicators of repeated economic crises, which appear to be the origins of the demographic crises revealed by the birth and death curves. Where in most cases the birth rate clearly exceeded the death rate between 1730 and 1770, from 1770 until 1790 a surplus of deaths is often observable. The demographic curves thus reproduce the sawteeth of the price curve and confirm the existence of serious and profound crises. The shape of the price curve in Western Europe has been explained by variation of the imports of precious metals. The discovery of gold in Brazil in the Minas Gerães and its introduction into European monetary circulation brought an increase in prices after 1730. The slowing of gold shipments around 1770 is one of the causes of the slackening of the increase in prices and hence of the economic stagnation.

Although wages increased, they lagged far behind prices, so that wage-earners—farm laborers, artisans, and factory hands—found themselves in a less favorable situation. In France prices increased on the average from 48 to 65 percent between 1730 and 1789, but wages rose only from 11 to 26 percent. Comparing the rise of *nominal wages* with the increase in the cost of living, we observe a fall in *real wages*. This fall was the consequence on the one hand of the rapid increase in the population of working age and on the other hand of the weak development of big industry in France. In fact, Watt's steam engine, perfected in England between 1769 and 1776, was not put to use in France until 1785 at the metallurgical factory of Le Creusot. The smelting of iron ore by means of coke instead of charcoal was practiced in England and Germany as early as 1750, but not before 1785 in France. Where the British textile industry used 20,000 jennies in 1789, France possessed only 7,000. In the last decade of the eighteenth century, England had numerous factories employing more than a hundred workers, but France had only a few—several metallurgical plants in Le Nord, Alsace, Lorraine, and Le Creusot. Western Germany and Belgium were perhaps better equipped than France, but northern Italy was definitely behind France. At the end of the eighteenth century, England had at least a twenty years' head start over the most developed countries on the continent.

The transformation of agriculture as recommended by the English agronomists and the French and Italian physiocrats did not create new jobs for the excess population. On the contrary, extension of pasturage, development of artificial meadows, enclosures, partition of common lands, and suppression of open grazing had the inevitable consequence of reducing the number of farm jobs. Livestock raising requires fewer hands than tilling the soil. When communal lands and open grazing were abolished, the poor *brassier* could no longer keep a cow or sheep and was reduced to the status of a rural proletarian. The modernization of agriculture therefore had the result of increasing the number of available workers. In England most of them were rapidly absorbed by industry, then in the process of rapid expansion. On the continent they were driven into unemployment and destitution and became elements of social disorder.

International trade also felt the effect of these changes. England became an even more intense competitor in the great international markets, clashing sharply with France especially. French merchants hoped to find compensation in increased trade with the United States, as seemed to be promised by the treaty of 1778, but they were disappointed. Instead of opening new outlets to French trade, the Anglo-French treaty of commerce of 1787 (the "Eden treaty") merely increased English exports to France and hence the economic struggle between the two countries.

In America the situation was somewhat different. The economic cycle does not seem to have developed there as it did in Europe, although the problems of employment and economic competition were similar. In the second half of the eighteenth century the local aristocracy tended to monopolize the land and to assemble vast estates, in particular in the Hudson valley. The surplus population resulting from the excess of births and the arrival of immigrants had difficulty in finding land in already cleared regions. The land-seeker had to go West as a pioneer. As for the merchants, the numerous fiscal measures adopted by the British government after 1763, especially the tax on tea, cut into their trade and drove them into opposition. In summary, after 1770, in America as in Europe, the economic cycle was unfavorable, increasing general insecurity and encouraging social agitation. . . .

The Atlantic Revolution also had political causes. The slow but continuous rise of prices during the course of the eighteenth century affected not only individuals but also the states. The financial resources of governments, coming essentially from taxes, rapidly became insufficient to cover their expenses. This was all the more true because expenses rose considerably as a result of the great wars that disturbed the first two-thirds of the eighteenth century. From 1700 to 1783 there took place the War of the Spanish Succession, which lasted twelve years, the War of the Polish Succession, which lasted four, the War of the Austrian Succession, which lasted seven, and the Seven Years' War: in all a total of thirty years of war out of sixty-three, or almost one year out of every two. The states had to introduce new taxes in order to meet their enormous military expenses. But nowhere was it possible to demand more of the peasants and the bourgeois, who until then had borne the principal share of government expenditures. It became imperative to abolish the fiscal privileges of the nobility and the clergy. Although this meant a frontal attack on privileged institutions, most sovereigns did not hesitate to adopt this policy. To justify their conduct, they employed the theories of those philosophes who sang the praises of absolute monarchy provided it was "enlightened." Thus "enlightened despotism" was born. It was characteristic particularly of the reigns of Frederick II in Prussia, Catherine II in Russia, Maria Theresa and Joseph II in the Holy Roman Empire (Germany), and sovereigns of lesser importance in Italy and Spain.

In a majority of states the aristocracy organized (in Montesquieu's phrase) in "intermediate corporations" resisted this policy of the enlightened despots, which tended to strengthen the power of the state and to diminish or even to abolish totally the aristocrats' privileges. Russia and the Ottoman Empire were the only countries in Europe that were not the arena of such struggles. This was a consequence of the social structure of these states: the weakness of the nobility and the bourgeoisie, which were badly organized, and the huge numbers of the peasantry, who were subject to unlimited burdens of taxation and labor services. In most other countries of Europe and the European colonies of America, the privileged corporations, in the name of the "historic rights" which Montesquieu

100

defended, resisted the demands of the state. In Sweden it was the Riksdag, composed of the representatives of the four orders (nobility, clergy, bourgeoisie, peasantry), with the aristocracy predominant, which opposed the monarchy until the coup d'état of King Gustavus III in 1772. In Poland, Bohemia, and Hungary the diets, composed only or almost only of the nobles and the bishops, relentlessly resisted every effort to reinforce the central power, to make the executive more powerful, and to modernize the administration of the state. In Prussia there existed no national diet but only provincial assemblies (*Landtäge*), in which the nobility held the preponderant influence; they too attempted to struggle against the claims of the monarch. In Italy the aristocracy dominated most of the states. In old republics like Venice and Genoa they ruled as they pleased, but where the states were headed by princes, as in Lombardy and Tuscany, they opposed the princes' reforms. The situation was similar in most of the German principalities, in the Austrian Netherlands and in the United Provinces. In France the aristocracy was the master of the *parlements,* the courts of justice which claimed the right to present their views on all legislative enactments. They also dominated the provincial Estates which still existed in Languedoc, Brittany, and Burgundy. Even in Great Britain the aristocracy remained very powerful in Parliament. The assemblies of the English colonies of North America represented primarily the local aristocracy. The great administrative bodies of the French colonies in the Antilles were in the hands of the privileged classes, and in the Spanish colonies the *cabildos* were likewise composed of aristocrats.

In all these countries—that is, throughout the West—the aristocracy formed a front against the claims of the sovereigns. They strove not only to maintain their position but also to improve it, by obtaining confirmation of their privileges and monopolies, by having land registers brought up to date, and by more harshly than ever requiring from their vassals recognition of their privileges and payment of the feudal dues owed to them (for they too were the victims of the price rise and needed more money). This attitude of the nobility has been studied especially in France, where it has been called the "aristocratic reaction," the "reaction of the nobility," and the "feudal reaction." But the aristocratic reaction was not a specifically French phenomenon; it was a phenomenon of the West as a whole.

The sovereigns first attempted to break the aristocratic reaction by traditional means—that is, by decrees and commands and by invoking their theoretical omnipotence. But the interests at stake were such that the resistance of the privileged classes became more and more stubborn. The sovereigns then gave thought to the counsels of philosophes of the Voltairean tendency, who held all subjects to be equal before the monarch, and they sought the alliance of the Third Estate against the privileged orders. In France, Louis XV suppressed the parlements in 1771 upon the advice of his ministers Maupeou, Terray, and D'Aiguillon, and reformed the fiscal system by placing slightly greater burdens upon the privileged groups. In Sweden Gustavus III amended the constitution by his own authority in 1772; he reduced the powers of the aristocratic Riksdag and governed with the support of the bourgeoisie and the peasantry. In the Hapsburg states, Maria Theresa compelled the "constituted corporations" of Austria, Bohemia, the southern Netherlands, and Lombardy to accept heavier taxation and a new customs tariff in 1775. In 1765 the British government extended the Stamp Act to its possessions of North America without consulting the colonial assemblies. Faced by their resistance, the king withdrew the Stamp Act the next year, but he affirmed the superiority of the Crown over the colonial assemblies by the Declaratory Act. In the same period Louis XV also proclaimed his authority over the French parlements, the citadels of the aristocracy, in the famous "flagellation" session.

If sovereigns sought the support of the people, the privileged orders did not hesitate to do so too. Outbidding the rulers, the aristocrats proclaimed themselves to be the only defenders of the people. In France the members of the parlements took the name of "Fathers of the People." For a dozen years the bourgeoisie sincerely believed that they had no better defenders than the parlements; not until 1788 did the duplicity of the parlements become apparent. In the English colonies of America, the assemblies sought support against the British sovereign among the merchants, small farmers, and artisans. In general the people were encouraged not only by the philosophes but also by the privileged orders to enter into struggle against the sovereign. In most countries of the West the "aristocratic reaction" inevitably led to a revolt of the nobility and soon thereafter to a revolt of the people.

No one who remembers the 1960s needs to be convinced that war has impact. Nor has any military conflict lacked its historians, for war—as Thomas Hardy once observed—makes "rattling good history." Yet too often one considers war's effects simply in terms of lives lost, physical damage done, and diplomatic consequences effected. As **GORDON WRIGHT** (b. 1912) demonstrates in the following selection on World War II, the changes wrought by war are far wider. Indeed, for reasons of space the excerpt below omits a portion of Wright's analysis—his treatment of the war's effects on intellectual and cultural life. Why have historians, who have shown such mastery in describing the conflicts themselves, been generally less successful in assessing the full imprint of war on society?

WAR: *The Impact of Total War*

Every modern war, someone has said, is also a revolution. It could hardly be otherwise; the stress and strain of total and protracted conflict unavoidably works profound changes in men and institutions. Some might argue that for the most part, these changes represent no drastic shift in direction, but only a speeding up of trends already under way in the prewar years. Yet even when existing processes are merely hastened, the unsettling impact may produce results equal to those of major revolutions. Neither the boatman nor the historian can afford to ignore "the difference in character and consequence between a gentle current and a cataract." ... No scientist, no historian has yet discovered a technique for measuring the enduring aftereffects of war; but no thoughtful man can doubt their severity or their persistence.... "No protracted war," Tocqueville once wrote, "can fail to endanger the freedom of a

From Gordon Wright, *The Ordeal of Total War, 1939–1945* (New York: Harper & Row, 1968), 234–37, 243–54, 263–67. Copyright © 1968 by Gordon Wright. Reprinted with permission of the publisher. Footnotes omitted.

democratic country.... War does not always give over democratic communities to military government, but it must invariably and immeasurably increase the powers of civil government; it must almost compulsorily concentrate the direction of all men and the management of all things in the hands of the administration. If it does not lead to despotism by sudden violence, it prepares men for it more gently by their habits. All those who seek to destroy the liberties of a democratic nation ought to know that war is the surest and the shortest means to accomplish it."

Tocqueville's dictum, appropriate enough in his own day, is even more applicable in the twentieth century. When nations must mobilize their total resources for a long struggle, the normal tensions between authority and liberty are intensified, and the trend toward dictatorship affects even the most democratic of nations. Where parliaments survive, their usual functions are sharply restricted; decision-making becomes increasingly concentrated in the hands of a small executive group, or even in those of one man.

Such had been the experience of the European nations during the First World War; such was even more clearly the case during the Second....

Wars leave their mark not only on political structures, but on every aspect of human organization. Indeed, their effects on social structures may be even deeper and more durable. On the other hand, measuring those effects is clearly more difficult; for societies are complex things, and the changes that occur may reveal themselves only gradually, well after the last shot is fired.

One obvious effect of total mobilization is a certain militarizing of society, at least for the duration of the war. The long strain calls for intensified social discipline: a greater regimentation of the citizen's life, a more hierarchical set of relationships, a partial replacement of civilian by military values. The altered demands of war also bring sharp changes in mores and in social values; new kinds of achievement are highly honored and yield fame and status, while others are pushed into the background. The normal channels of social mobility are twisted or blocked as by an earthquake, and new channels are suddenly wrenched open for heretofore obscure citizens. A reordering of social relationships inevitably follows—sometimes in the direction of greater leveling, sometimes in the direction of increased inequalities. As a rule, the chief social benefits of modern war have gone to the professional soldier at the expense of those who practice the peacetime arts. Midway through the First World War, the German officer Wilhelm Groener rather smugly remarked: "The uniform counts more among us now than the black coat of the civilian, and the cry for dictatorship by the military is raised on every side." Early in the Second World War, an American social scientist somberly predicted that the conflict would produce a world of "garrison states" in which the "specialists in violence" would fix a durable grip on societies everywhere.

Some of the foregoing changes did occur in Europe during the Second World War—though with particular nuances from one society to another, and with some rather surprising aberrations. One notable fact was that while the usual militarizing of society did occur in the broad sense of that term, it failed to put the military into the saddle anywhere, and in one case even reduced the political and social authority enjoyed by the armed forces. That case was Germany. During the war of 1914–1918, the German military had fixed its grip on almost every aspect of domestic life, from political decision-making to industrial production, food rationing, labor policy, the control of public information, and censorship. After 1939, the armed forces found themselves excluded from all such functions, and even from such responsibilities as the raising and training of reserves. Just as Hitler himself increasingly monopolized the strategic and even the operational conduct of the war, so the various agencies of the Nazi party absorbed all domestic administrative tasks—police and security, manpower allocation, psychological mobilization and indoctrination. "The Fuehrer," wrote Goebbels in 1943, "is totally opposed to the Wehrmacht engaging in tasks that are not germane to it.... The Wehrmacht is to limit itself to conducting the war in a military sense and to leave everything else to civilians." If the conflict further increased Germany's "garrison state" qualities, it did so at the expense and not to the advantage of the professional soldier. The traditional prestige of the German officer corps, and its assumption of a dominant role in past wars, worked against the army at a time when the nation's new political elite jealously refused to share authority with any potential rival.

In the Soviet Union, on the other hand, the war did bring a carefully controlled shift in status and authority to the advantage of the military. The vast influx of Soviet citizens into the armed forces after 1941, and the Kremlin's increased dependence on the generals' courage and loyalty, assured the soldiers of greater deference and higher status. But although honors and praise were dealt out generously, the officer corps was given no expanded role outside the sphere of military operations; the tasks of social control and of adapting Soviet society to wartime needs were exclusively reserved to the political elite. Even though the bloodiest fighting and the greatest destruction of the war occurred on the Russian front, the war's effects on the Soviet political system and social structure were probably slighter than in any other participating country. For unlike the Western democracies, the Soviet Union had already become a garrison state before the war; and unlike Germany, the Soviet Union did not have to face the postwar social upheaval caused by defeat.

One would expect the war to have had a far greater impact on the liberal societies of the West, where the transition from peace to war was bound to be more unsettling. Such was indeed the case; yet the changes were not always the ones that might have been predicted. The apparent shift toward a garrison state in Great Britain (the only western European nation to endure the long strain of protracted war as an independent belligerent) brought increased status and authority to the military, but not at the expense of civilian officialdom or of the civilian population as a whole. Survival and victory depended on the united effort of the British people, whether in or out of uniform; total mobilization put everyone onto the front lines. Episodes like the Battle of Britain were peculiarly important in eroding the differences between civilians and soldiers. And when the war effort depended as much on the production and delivery of goods as on battlefield heroics, special privileges for men in uniform would have been difficult to justify.

The war brought, too, a drastic process of leveling, a kind of flattening of the social pyramid. British leadership had no choice but to practice what someone has called "demostrategy"; it implied an intensified state concern for the health and morale of the whole population. From the early months of the war, the government ordered a marked broadening of social services provided to all citizens, regardless of class or military status. The emergency evacuation of millions of women and children from Greater London suddenly brought to light a number of social deficiencies of which few Britons had been consciously aware. It was clear that the nation's hospital facilities were desperately inadequate, and that hundreds of thousands of urban refugee children had in the past been inadequately fed, clothed, and cared for. The government introduced a whole series of emergency welfare measures; but more important still, the conditions of war stimulated a nationwide mood of reform. From this mood emerged the welfare-state concept in its modern form. So great was its appeal that when Sir William Beveridge issued his famous report in 1943, outlining a postwar plan for universal social security, the bulky and austere document became an overnight best seller; queues of citizens stood before bookstores to get their copies.

Wartime government controls contributed, too, to the leveling process. Critical shortages of consumer goods after 1940 forced an austerity standard for all; and changing mores reinforced government regulations to impose a growing uniformity in standards of living, of dress, and of public conduct generally. Long years of war required rigorous social discipline, and such discipline was made more bearable when it was shared by everyone. Yet along with the flattening of the social pyramid, there occurred a marked increase in social mobility. New opportunities were opened to many men and women whose roles had been humble or obscure in peacetime. The rise of the scientists was perhaps the most striking example. Only a few years before the war, a British cabinet minister had remarked condescendingly, "What I like about scientists is that they are a team, so that one need not know their names." Suddenly, in the war years, the names of certain scientists came to be almost as well known among the cognoscenti as those of generals and ministers. On a broader scale, the rise of women in social status was equally notable. The increase in the number of British women employed in industry, government, and the armed forces exceeded that of any other warring country; it profoundly altered the role and the self-image of British women. The new technological aspect of the war also had its effect (in Britain as elsewhere) in pushing forward men of technical and managerial talent, both in the government and in the armed services. Sir John Anderson, a highly skilled career civil servant without experience as a politician, held important cabinet posts throughout the war, and in 1945 was even nominated by Churchill to succeed to the prime ministership in case Churchill and Eden were killed en route to Yalta. Likewise, the new-style armed forces enabled the military managers to assert a right to equality with charismatic battlefield leaders.

Perhaps the most drastic immediate impact of the war on social structures occurred in the German-occupied countries of the Continent. Defeat and occupation radically transformed the dominant value-systems and the relationships among social groups. Some previously favored elements suddenly found themselves transformed into outsiders, threatened by physical destruction as well as social ruin. Others found the channels of upward mobility suddenly opened wide to those who were opportunistically inclined. In areas like Poland and occupied Russia, the conquerors consciously endeavored to liquidate the whole intellectual and professional elite, and to substitute an imported German ruling class. In western Europe, favors often went to men who had been disgruntled misfits or frustrated failures in their prewar societies. But the deeper social effects in the occupied countries were aftereffects, to be felt during the postwar years. For the nucleus of a new elite gradually emerged from the various resistance movements; its members were catapulted after 1944 into positions of political, economic, and social prominence to which only a few of them could have aspired without the upheaval of the war. Nowhere were they to attain a monopoly of postwar power or status; many would be shunted back into obscurity after a few months or years of fleeting notoriety. But the long-range effect was to produce a kind of circulation of the elites, out of which would come an amalgam of old-established and newly-arrived elements in roles of authority and status.

In the defeated Axis nations, too, the social effects of the war were mainly aftereffects; but the impact was no less profound for being delayed. Germany and Italy had already undergone a partial social revolution during the prewar years—a revolution that had brought the new Fascist or Nazi party elite into uneasy partnership with those elements of the older elites that chose to collaborate. In Germany, a radical wing of the Nazi movement had favored a much more sweeping social revolution that would liquidate most of the older elite and would culminate in a thoroughly totalitarian system. This impulse was strongest within the SS, some of whose leaders talked of creating an "SS-state" in which all the key positions would be monopolized by members of that elite formation. The war did bring an impressive growth in the size and influence of the SS, but at the same time forced postponement of its leaders' ambitions. So long as the fighting lasted, they concentrated their energies on the task of creating and consolidating a German empire in the east, while deferring their domestic goals for implementation after victory was won.

But the social revolution that eventually followed Germany's defeat was to be of a quite different sort. The destruction of much of the Nazi elite, the temporary disgrace of those powerful elements that had collaborated with Hitler, and the massive influx of a huge uprooted refugee population from the east were to produce a kind of social disintegration out of which a largely new social order would eventually emerge. The refugees (mostly from Protestant regions) were scattered in camps throughout the western zones of occupied Germany, and many eventually settled in what had been solidly Catholic areas. The effect was a somewhat greater religious and social "homogenization" of the western zones. On the other hand, the permanent division of Germany that split off the heavily Protestant eastern part led to a sharp increase of Catholic influence in the segment that eventually came to be governed from Bonn.

Still more profound were the social changes that emerged from the massive physical destruction of the country, and from the disastrous blows suffered by the old ruling elites. The rebuilding of the German economy opened the way to the creation, for the first time in German history, of a thoroughly capitalist system in place of the old uneasy mixture of industrial capitalism and quasi-feudal traditionalism. The industrial-managerial group rapidly emerged as the unchallenged upper stratum of society, able to assert its individualistic, competitive values as those of the new Germany. Greater social mobility, a personal success ideology, and a somewhat exaggerated materialism seemed on the way to replacing the more rigid and status-ridden order of the past. What kind of amalgam would eventually emerge remained somewhat uncertain, but it was clear enough that the war had opened the way to a quite unintended kind of social revolution in Germany.

That modern war strains and disrupts the political, social, and economic fabric of a highly organized continent is too obvious to be doubted. Its effects on the psychological fabric are much more controversial. Common sense and experience testify that an individual may be traumatized by a shattering personal experience; and certainly millions of individual Europeans suffered some kind of traumatic experience during the Second World War. But whether whole societies may be traumatized by a collectively experienced catastrophe is more open to debate. Those who believe that com-

109

munities of men possess a kind of collective mind or psychological fabric will be more likely to seek out and to accept evidence of the generalized impact of disaster. Yet even those who are skeptical of the idea of "socially-shared psychopathology" will recognize that the long strain and the terrifying climaxes of modern war must leave their mark on tens of thousands of survivors.

Such evidence as emerged from the Second World War relates not to entire populations but to special groups: members of the armed forces, children separated from their families, prisoners of war, civilians subjected to heavy bombing raids, and concentration camp inmates. The data, though extensive, is spotty, and rarely permits confident generalization. Only the Americans and the British compiled information and made studies of psychological responses during the war itself; as for the data from Germany, most of it was gathered immediately after the war by American teams, or was contributed by survivors of the concentration camps. Probably the surest conclusions are those that concern the short- and long-range effects of mass bombing.

The approach of war had inspired panicky fears in Britain and France about the anticipated consequences of air attacks. The British Air Ministry estimated that air-raid casualties during the early weeks of war would run into the millions, and would produce widespread neurosis and panic. Indeed, a committee of psychiatrists had predicted in 1938 that psychological casualties might exceed physical injuries by a ratio of three to one, so that the former might approach three or four million cases during the first six months. When war was declared, therefore, more than three million women and children were hastily evacuated from Greater London to the country districts or to smaller towns. When the expected air raids failed to materialize, the majority of the refugees found their own way back to London. By the time the German blitz of 1940–1941 began, the initial panic had passed. This time there was no organized evacuation; many Londoners preferred the risks of bombing to the dislocation and tensions of life as unwelcome guests in a crowded rural or small-town home. In fact, there is fairly persuasive evidence that children suffered more severely from the psychological effects of separation from their families than from the rigors of the air raids.

The impact of the bombing, when it came at last, seemed to belie the fears and predictions of the experts. There was no mass

110

hysteria, no social disruption inspired by panic or shock. The nearest approach to spontaneous mass action or "civil disobedience" was the occupation of London subway stations by thousands of citizens who lacked air-raid shelters. Civil defense officials worked tirelessly and efficiently to care for the injured, to clear street obstructions, and to restore disrupted public utilities. There was no increase in the number of mental disorders reported; the number of suicides and of arrests for drunkenness or disorderly conduct actually decreased during the war years. On the other hand, cases diagnosed as "temporary traumatic neurosis" were frequent in heavily-bombed areas, and increased absenteeism from work on grounds of illness often followed an air attack. There was also a rise in the incidence of such psychosomatic disorders as peptic ulcers in bombed areas.

Fortunately for the British, the air blitz tapered off after about ten months, and there was a long respite before the period of V-1 and V-2 attacks in 1944. No doubt this interlude reduced the nervous strain in British cities, and helped to keep the number of psychological casualties low. Meanwhile, the Germans were beginning to confront a steadily intensifying barrage of air raids both more severe and more protracted than anything the British—or any other people heretofore—had known. Here, too, the experience seemed to prove the remarkable capacity of human beings to bear up under unprecedented strain and terror. As in England, there was neither mass panic nor social disruption (save in a few instances when the municipal authorities failed to respond effectively to emergency conditions following an air raid). Even in the massive Hamburg raids, which laid waste half the city and left 48 percent of the population homeless, the effect was widespread shock rather than mass hysteria or economic breakdown. Berlin, which underwent the longest period of almost uninterrupted raids (eighteen months) and which by 1945 was reduced largely to rubble, continued to function as an organized community until the very end. In Germany as in England there seems to have been no increase in the number of mental disorders. But here, too, the number of ulcer cases rose in bombed areas, and work absenteeism was more common after raids. Signs of tension and strain were general; the German authorities finally had to abandon the use of air-raid sirens to warn against isolated attacks, in an effort to reduce fatigue caused by unnecessary alarm.

The remarkable resilience of both the English and the Germans

111

when subjected to intense air warfare blasted the prewar myth about the devastating effects of terror bombing; but perhaps it tended to create a new myth in place of the old. It was easy to conclude, during and after the war, that mass bombing had been a relatively ineffective weapon, and that its psychological effect had actually been to improve the morale of an attacked population, to intensify its will to resist. Such a conclusion can be neither affirmed nor denied on the basis of the evidence from the Second World War. Even though mass hysteria did not occur, there was widespread shock that amounted to temporary traumatic neurosis, and that produced a kind of numb indifference rather than a heightened determination to fight and win. As for the long-range consequences of these temporary psychological disorders, the evidence is scanty. One British study of mental cases carried out in 1948 showed only 3 percent of this sample to be clearly connected with air-raid experience during the war. It is quite possible, however, that hidden damage of a deeper sort went undetected.

The psychological impact of the war on members of the armed forces is difficult to assess, since only the British and the Americans kept detailed statistics. British psychiatric casualties seem to have averaged about 10 percent of total battle casualties; but this average concealed a wide variation, ranging from 2 to 30 percent, depending on the particular conditions and the duration of a given battle. Long periods of severe strain produced serious effects. For example, in the garrison at Malta, under intense air bombardment in 1942–1943, more than one man in four eventually showed some kind of pathological response. In 1940, a ship loaded with exhausted and demoralized British troops who had fought in the French campaign was sunk near Bordeaux, and the soldiers dumped into a sea coated with flaming oil; every man who was rescued suffered severe psychological aftereffects. Many of the Dunkirk survivors reached home in a state of total neurotic collapse, "suffering from acute hysteria, reactive depression, functional loss of memory or of the use of their limbs, and a variety of other psychiatric symptoms...."

During the First World War, all such disorders had been lumped under the misleading label "shell shock," and it was assumed that such men were either weaklings or cowards. At best, they had been given a spell of rest and then sent back to the front lines, where they often broke down completely, and became incurable casualties. This mistake was corrected in the Second World

War by improved understanding and better methods of treatment. Both the British and the Americans soon learned that it was essential to treat acute hysteria cases as quickly as possible, before the abnormal behavior patterns had time to become stabilized in the nervous system. They learned, too, that to send "cured" neurotics back into action was almost always futile, and that a transfer or a discharge was the only alternative to permanent damage. They learned, finally, that not only weaklings were susceptible to psychological battle disorders; that "practically everyone has his neurotic breaking point if the stresses are severe enough." The advance of psychiatric knowledge had at least one clearly favorable result: it sharply reduced the number of permanent psychological casualties in the British and American armed forces, as compared to the record of 1914–1918.

No experience of strain and terror during the Second World War exceeded that of the men and women confined in German concentration camps. Inadequate food, brutal treatment, harsh labor assignments, constant uncertainty about the future seem to have produced radical personality changes in many inmates. The program of calculated terror used by the SS guards was evidently designed to strip the prisoner of all human traits, to destroy his self-respect, to "depersonalize" him. The effect of the treatment varied widely: regression toward infantile traits was perhaps the commonest result, while others managed some sort of adaptation in order to survive. In most cases, the central concern after the first few weeks came to be self-preservation; all other values faded before this urge to live, no matter what the cost. Some long-time prisoners even came to model themselves after the SS guards, and to ape their conduct and values. Only a few managed to cling, despite the inhuman conditions in the camp, to those altruistic traits that mark normal human conduct. The enduring effects of the concentration camp experience were to be demonstrated after the war by the frequency of psychological disorders among former inmates. Chronic anxiety and panic were frequent, while certain mental and physical diseases that occurred ten or twenty years later have been diagnosed as the result of brain injury caused by malnutrition and prolonged, intense fear experienced during the concentration camp years.

The full breadth and depth of the war's psychological impact on the peoples of Europe will, of course, never be measured. At least one psychiatrist, on returning to the Continent in 1945, contended that almost every inhabitant of occupied Europe showed some traits that might be described as neurotic or even psychotic. Others spoke of a new set of impenetrable "psychological boundaries" that would henceforth separate those with sharply differing sets of wartime experiences. Still others spoke with a touch of awe of the unexpected power of adaptation shown by ordinary human beings in time of crisis. On the surface, Europe after the end of the war seemed to return quite rapidly to a kind of normalcy, and its citizens a decade later no longer appeared to be haunted by the terrible memory of their wartime experiences. Yet who is to say whether deeper lesions may not have persisted, marring and distorting the psyche of the "normal" European who survived the conflict? "Perhaps," suggests Richard M. Titmuss, "more lasting harm was wrought to the minds and to the hearts of men, women and children than to their bodies. The disturbances to family life, the separation of mothers and fathers from their children, of husbands from their wives, of pupils from their schools, of people from their recreation, of society from the pursuits of peace—perhaps all of these indignities of war have left wounds which will take time to heal and infinite patience to understand." Thucydides remarked long ago that ". . . war, which takes away the comfortable provision of daily life, is a hard master and tends to assimilate men's characters to their conditions." It may be that characters warped by the experience of protracted total war will never quite return to their former shape, and that from these warped qualities may emerge the neuroses of the next generation. . . .

Amidst discussion of the vast impersonal forces that mold history, one sometimes forgets that history is made by men and women. The difficult question is not whether men and women are the actors in history; of course they are. The problem is whether these actors, like those in a play, are carrying out a plot whose outcome they will not affect, or whether, like actors in an improvisation, they can decisively change the outcome. **SIDNEY HOOK** (b. 1902), a philosopher much interested in history, has discerningly explored the "Great Man" theory in his book, *The Hero in History*. In the following excerpt, Hook states the case for considering Lenin a hero, that is, a man who significantly shaped the course of history. What objections might one lodge against this interpretation?

LEADERS: *The Hero in History*

However we assess the causal significance of the Russian Revolution for subsequent European development, we must face the position which asserts that the October Revolution was inevitable. The term "inevitable" in this connection is ambiguous. Even those who use it do not mean it literally. What they do mean is that, given its social and economic antecedents, the October Revolution was overwhelmingly the most likely of all the relevant historical possibilities. This is the view of the orthodox Marxists of the Leninist persuasion. It is a view, however, that can be held independently of their political program and certainly demands consideration.

The denial that the Russian Revolution was inevitable in the light of Russian social and economic development entails the belief that some other factor was of primary importance. On our hy-

From Sidney Hook, *The Hero in History* (New York: Humanities Press, 1943), 200–210, 220–228. Reprinted with permission of the author and publisher. Footnotes omitted.

pothesis this factor was the presence of an event-making individual —Lenin. Those who uphold the thesis of inevitability admit that Lenin's presence may have been necessary as far as the *calendar date* of the Russian Revolution was concerned, but, in conformity with their general philosophy of history, affirm that even without him "it would necessarily have come sooner or later." Since our denial of the inevitability of the Russian Revolution is made on the grounds that an event-making personality decided the issue, and that in his absence from the scene events would have fallen out quite differently with profoundly different consequences to the world, the second and third steps of our argument will be considered together.

The contention that the Russian Revolution was historically inevitable rests upon two main lines of evidence. The first consists in the accumulation of data which indicate that, although Russia was predominately a backward agricultural country, she also possessed a highly developed industry with a class conscious proletariat. The standing need of the Russian peasants for land, the dislocations in industry produced by the war, the prevalent mood of war-weariness, and the disorganization of the governmental apparatus produced a revolutionary situation which became progressively more acute from February to the eve of October. A revolutionary situation, however, is not yet a revolution. For that a political party is needed. The second line of evidence is then introduced. This consists in showing that the Bolshevik Party, and the Bolshevik Party alone, had the correct program to meet the needs and demands of the great masses of the Russian people. Taken together, the revolutionary situation and party made the October Revolution the only possible historical solution.

Even if nothing in the above account were disputed, the conclusion is a *non sequitur.* There have been other periods in history which showed us a revolutionary situation and a revolutionary party with a "correct" program from its point of view—and the whole summed up to failure—for example, Germany in 1923. Nor is it true that the Bolshevist Party was the only party with the program which, on this analysis, was called for by the situation. The Bolshevik program was really adapted from the official program of the Social Revolutionary Party during this period.

The great difference was that the program of the Social Revolutionary Party remained a paper resolution, completely disre-

116

garded by its representatives in the Provisional Government and Soviets, while the Bolshevik Party carried the program out.

Given the situation in Russia, the October Revolution must be regarded as the work of the Bolshevik Party which capitalized for its own political purposes the hunger of the Russian masses for peace, land, and bread. The main problem then is the relation of Lenin to the Bolshevik Party—to its program, strategy, tactics, and will to action. Before we consider it, we should observe that, in fact, the leading role of the Bolshevik Party in the events that culminated in the seizure of power is disputed by none. In question is only the extent to which the Bolshevik Party influenced the restless mood of the Russian masses. Miliukov, typical of the historians of the right, holds their agitation largely responsible for the existence of the mass attitudes which they thereupon skillfully exploited. Trotsky, typical of the historians of the left, maintains that the Bolsheviks from first to last lagged behind the temper of the workers and peasants. Kerensky, speaking for the center, asserts that "the psychology of absolute distrust for the authorities" was aroused in the masses primarily by the attempted *coup d'état* of Kornilov, aided by the friends of Miliukov; the Bolsheviks did the rest. But no matter how the mood of the Russian masses was created, it did not make the Russian Revolution. That was the work of the Bolshevik Party.

But without Nicolai Lenin the work of the Bolshevik Party from April to October 1917 is unthinkable. Anyone who familiarizes himself with its internal history will discover that objectives, policy, slogans, controlling strategy, day-by-day tactics were laid down by Lenin. Sometimes he counseled in the same painstaking way that a tutor coaches a spirited but bewildered pupil; sometimes he commanded like an impatient drill sergeant barking at a raw recruit. But from first to last it was Lenin. Without him there would have been no October Revolution. Here is the evidence.

a. Until Lenin's return to Russia on April 3, and his presentation of his thesis of April 4, the Bolshevik Party and its official organ were supporting the Provisional Government of Kerensky. Lenin's April Theses, which called for the overthrow of this government by armed insurrection and for all power to the Soviets, came as a bombshell in his own party.

Speaking of the position of the Bolshevik Party in Russia before Lenin arrived, Joseph Stalin wrote on November 19, 1924:

This position was utterly erroneous, for it begot pacifist illusions, poured water on the mill of defensism and hampered the revolutionary education of the masses. In those days I shared this erroneous position with other Party comrades, and completely renounced it only in the middle of April, when I endorsed Lenin's thesis.

At the beginning Lenin was absolutely alone in his stand. His intransigent demand for immediate cessation of the war against Germany, his call "to turn the imperialist war into a civil war," outraged all political parties. It played into the hands of his enemies who desperately sought to pin on him the false label of "German agent." Nonetheless, before the month was out Lenin had converted the executive committee and the most active spirits of his party. Before his arrival the local Bolsheviks were seriously considering organic fusion with the Mensheviks. Lenin changed all that. He drew a sharp line of division between his own party and all the other working-class parties that refused to accept his program.

The significance of Lenin's work in arming his party with a new set of objectives may be gauged by the fact that this involved abandoning doctrines the Bolsheviks had firmly held for an entire decade. Until the February Revolution, all Bolsheviks, including Lenin, believed in what they called "the democratic dictatorship of the workers and peasants." The task of this regime would be to carry out in Russia the achievements of the democratic revolutions of the west. In 1917 Lenin changed his position and that of his party. The Russian Revolution was to be the first breach in the world economy of capitalism. It was to be a "dictatorship of the proletariat" that would stimulate similar dictatorships in the west which cooperatively would initiate the transition to world socialism.

His opponents predicted that Lenin's program would not appease the hunger of the Russian masses for peace, land, and bread; that world-wide socialist revolutions would not follow upon the dictatorship of the proletariat in Europe; that Russia would be devastated by civil war and chaos; that the autocracy of the Czarist bureaucrats and landlords would be replaced by an even more ruthless autocracy of Bolshevik bureaucrats. Despite all criticism from without as well as within his own party, Lenin won his way without yielding an inch.

b. Once Lenin had converted his party to the program of civil war and armed insurrection against the democratic Provisional Government, the main task was clear. It was to choose the proper moment to strike. Until that moment, Lenin was careful to exploit the status of legality in order to carry on his propaganda for over-throw, and to accumulate weapons. After the abrupt turn had been made from critical collaboration to outright opposition, it was not easy to restrain the Bolshevik rank and file, its periphery and sympathizers, from precipitating matters prematurely. If one shoots at a king, one must not miss. And if an insurrection is begun, it is death to fail. Lenin, therefore, was compelled to keep a very close check on the more exuberant of his followers as well as on the mass outbursts that rose periodically as a consequence of delay in meeting the urgent, immediate demands of workers and peasants. He had to forestall an attempt to seize power when the chances were un-favorable for winning it, or holding it after it was won.

During the June days, and much more so during early July, extremist sentiment was rife in influential sections of the Petrograd working class and military garrison. Even some of the Bolshevik leaders were toying with the idea of giving the signal for an all-out attack against the Kerensky government. It was Lenin who held them back. He warned that they would be unable to finish what they started, that they would be crushed, and that the opportunity to strike for power would be lost, perhaps forever. Even so, a con-siderable number of workers got out of control and appeared on the streets with rifles in their hands. Although they had tried to call off this demonstration, which was largely the result of their previous agitation, the Bolshevik Party at Lenin's command placed itself at its head in order to prevent it from going over into open insurrection. The Bolsheviks were successful in this. But because the Party had taken public responsibility for the armed demonstration, their apparatus was forced underground and they suffered a con-siderable loss of political influence on the masses. They regained their influence and partially emerged from illegality only after Kornilov attempted his *coup d'état* from the right against the Kerensky government.

c. The most decisive period in Lenin's career of mastery over the Bolshevik Party was the very eve of the October Revolution.

119

Although in hiding, Lenin kept in close touch with the moods of the discontented soldiery and peasants. He was well informed of the disposition of military forces in and about the capital. The Central Committee of the Bolshevik Party, having learned the lesson of the July days, was inclined to go slow. The very furthest thing from their minds was the desire to go over to an open offensive when they received word from Lenin that it was *now or never.*

At first Lenin was in the minority. He raged and stormed. He threatened to go over their heads to the lower party functionaries and to organize matters without them. He wrote letters to influential party members to get them to bring pressure on the lagging executive committee. After fierce and stubborn debate, he won them to his position. How urgent Lenin considered the period they were in—as *the* period in which to stake all on a bid for power—is apparent from his letter of October 21, 1917, to the Central Executive Committee, demanding the organization of an armed insurrection during the next few days: "The success of both the Russian and world revolution depends upon two or three days of struggle." When he finally won his majority by a vote of ten to two, the die was cast. The Bolsheviks took state power.

d. That they kept state power during the subsequent year was again due primarily to Lenin's guiding policy. One group of the Central Committee desired to continue the war against Hohenzollern Germany while appealing to the German workers to emulate the Bolsheviks. Another group advocated the policy of "neither peace nor war." Lenin stood firm for a signed treaty of peace which would give the Bolsheviks respite from their foreign enemy for the moment and sufficient time to consolidate themselves against their internal foes. During these days, Lenin was again a hopeless minority at first but hammered away until his colleagues yielded. The Treaty of Brest-Litovsk was signed.

If Lenin had not returned to Russia or had died en route, there is no evidence whatsoever to support the hypothesis that Kamenev, Muranov, and Stalin, then in control of Bolshevik policy, would have reversed helm and taken up war to the end against the democratic provisional Government. If during June and July Lenin had not been present to prevail upon the excited spirits among the Bolsheviks and other *Enragés* and forestall an uprising, the whole organization would have been destroyed in blood. If, on the eve of October, the Bolsheviks had marked time despite Lenin's exhortations, Kerensky would have been able to garrison the capital with reliable troops and easily cope with the Bolsheviks. If Lenin had not stopped the Germans by giving them all they wanted, their army would have taken both Petrograd and Moscow, since military resistance was no longer possible. Lenin and his colleagues would either have met the fate of Karl Liebknecht and Rosa Luxemburg in Germany or would have been dispersed to the four corners of the vast Russian land.

Lenin, of course, was not the Bolshevik Party. But the Bolshevik Party became the instrument it did because of Lenin. It is doubtful whether any man before him ever wielded such power in a political party; certainly not in an organization that professed to be democratic or socialistic.

If Lenin had not been on the scene, not a single revolutionary leader could have substituted for him. Not Stalin, by his own confession. Not Zinoviev, Lenin's closest follower, who ran out on the October Revolution. Not Kamenev, whose mind Lenin changed at the same time he changed Stalin's, but who acted like Zinoviev. Not Trotsky. Although the record shows that Trotsky was the only outstanding Russian figure whose theoretical position and practical program were identical with those of Lenin *before* April 1917, he would have failed where Lenin succeeded. For one thing, he arrived in Russia a month after Lenin did. By that time Lenin had completed the reeducation of the Bolshevik Party. Trotsky would have had to do this, but he was not a member of the organization. His own party was numerically insignificant and relatively uninfluential. Finally, he owed whatever authority he enjoyed in the Bolshevik Party, which he joined in August, to Lenin's recognition of his capacities and Lenin's constant protection against the suspicion and opposition of the second-line Bolshevik leaders. Trotsky, alone, was doomed to failure because, despite his other great gifts, he lacked the organizational genius so necessary for political success. His imperious manner provoked people instead of reconciling them to his capacities. He could win an audience but, unlike Lenin, he could not win over party opponents. And he openly betrayed an impatience with mediocrity which no one forgives in a newcomer. . . .

What manner of man was Lenin who filled this event-making role in history? Under the circumstances, our curiosity is entirely legitimate, because it is the *character* of the individual which chiefly distinguishes the eventful man from the event-making man. What we are particularly interested in is discovering the combination of characteristics which gave Lenin political preeminence over a galaxy of individuals who as thinkers, writers, and mass orators displayed greater talents than he possessed. Analysis of this, as of any form of genius, is difficult to make. Particularly in politics, a medium in which virtues and vices, reason and stupidity, have an entirely different specific gravity than in the clear waters of personal relations and scientific activity, is it difficult to evaluate genius. No bare enumeration of character traits can do justice to the power of insight which flashes to the surface when these traits operate together in the context of problems, dangers, ideal goals.

One of the most conspicuous expressions of political insight is the sense of timing. Without it, great intelligence can be ineffective. Coupled with strong will, it can carry a mediocre mind to the heights. No one who knew, say, Plechanov and Stalin before February expected that one would fade out of the historical picture so soon and that the other would gradually emerge as the strong man of the strongest party. But it was Lenin's superb sense of political timing, nourished by an intelligence more practical than Plechanov's and a will more inflexible than Stalin's, that won an empire for the Bolsheviks.

Every adequate analysis of Lenin, the political man, must note his stubborn tenacity of purpose and unsurpassable confidence in himself. If he ever harbored a doubt about the ultimate success of his cause, the rightness of his tactical decisions, the high price of victory paid out in human suffering and injustice, he never expressed it to anyone. He was beyond the corruptions of pleasure and immune to the impractical delights of thought. His basic allegiance was to certain simple ideal socialist goals which were at the same time so vague that, given the consciousness of his own absolute integrity, he could always justify to himself what *he* did despite appearances.

Lenin could influence human beings only within the framework of organization. He had no power as an individual with the masses. Although unpretentious, he lacked the common touch which wins the masses by a radiant sympathy; and although he always had something to tell them, he could not strike the sparks of fire to inflame them into action.

Lenin was a party man. The life of the party was spiritual

meat and substance to him. Just as some men's personalities are sustained by a church, and others are enriched by the passions and crises and problems of love, family, and knowledge, so Lenin's personality was sustained by, and developed within, the party. He was never far from the center of any organization of which he was a member. In his own mind, wherever he was, *there* was the party. His passions, his problems, his judgments all reflect this intense concentration on the party—a concentration which was all the more selfless because subconsciously he was the party. Whether he considered problems of state or art or philosophy, there was not a disinterested nerve in his body. In fact, all problems were for him problems of politics, even the listening to music and the playing of chess.

Lenin was not merely a party man. He raised the party to the level of a political principle. This is the source of all his deviations from the essentially democratic views of Marx. For Marx, a political party was conceived as a kind of cross between an international educational institution for the working class and a pressure group, as something that would come and go and be reconstituted in the forge of historical events. But for Lenin the political party was an army of professional revolutionists. The organization of professional revolutionists was of supreme importance in capturing state power. Iron-clad control of organization was essential to victory. This ideal organization must, like Lenin himself, be acutely sensitive to the moods of the masses. It must have a perfect sense of timing. And above all, it must be imbued with the unshakable conviction that it knew what the true interests of the masses were, better than they did themselves. In the light of this knowledge, it was justified in promising them anything to get them to move, and in manipulating them into actions which, even if they were foredoomed to failure, would educate them up to a level of Bolshevik understanding. The professional revolutionist by definition was one who wanted nothing for himself, and in fact cared so little for material goods that he could sincerely believe that he was free from the temptations and corruptions of absolute power.

Lenin was a Marxist who interchanged the "dictatorship of the proletariat"—which for Marx was a *broader* democracy of the working class counterposed to the narrower democracy of capitalist society—with the outright dictatorship of a minority Communist Party *over* the proletariat. Lenin believed that the hope of man-

123

kind lay in the struggle of the working class to abolish capitalism and therewith all economic classes. But he was even more convinced that this struggle could be successful *only* when led by his own party no matter what its name. He did not flinch from the inexorable conclusion that, therefore, any individual or group who opposed *the* Party was objectively "an enemy of mankind."

At one stroke all other parties of the working class were thrust on the other side of the barricades. Lenin not only used the method of "amalgam" against them; he believed it. The method of amalgam was to link up a Kronstadt sailor fighting for Soviet democracy against party dictatorship with the Black Hundreds of Czarism, to identify a socialist critic of Bolshevism, who had languished for years in prerevolutionary prisons, with partisans of Denikin and Kolchak. Before Lenin died, *anyone* who called for Soviet democracy as opposed to party dictatorship was forthwith denounced as a counterrevolutionist. This seems ironical because Lenin's chief slogan against Kerensky had been "All Power to the Soviets." But Lenin would have failed to see any irony whatever in such a situation. Slogans, like people, had to be used in a functional or, to use his own expression, in a "concrete" way, that is, to carry forward the political task of the moment. The goal in behalf of which political tasks were to be solved was power for the Bolsheviks. Thus, when it seemed necessary for the victory of the party, Lenin proclaimed "All Power to the Soviets." In July, when it seemed that the Bolsheviks could not capture the Soviets, Lenin denounced the slogan and looked around for other agencies through which power could be won. Later, when the situation once more made the prospect of Bolshevik capture of the Soviets favorable, Lenin returned to the old slogan. But after power was won in October, Soviet democracy meant the possibility that the Bolsheviks might lose power. To Lenin this was plain counterrevolution.

Had he been consistent, Lenin would have also drawn the conclusion that anyone *within* his party who opposed his policies was also objectively an enemy of mankind. But he showed his genius by following not the logic of his position but the needs of successful organization. He displayed great aptitude in using and winning for his purposes those in his own ranks who disagreed with him. He could work with people who without him could not work with each other. It was left to Stalin to draw the logical conclusion, and to convict any opponent on any matter of being an enemy of humanity.

But that was when Lenin's party did not have to make a revolution.

In contrast to the entire field of his rivals in the period from February to October, Lenin knew what he wanted—power. In contrast to them, he knew how important a political army was and how it could best be deployed to achieve power. And in contrast to them once more, he dared all on his program and on himself. Like the good dialectical materialist he was, his faith was nothing short of cosmic. Compared to Lenin with his deep belief in himself as an instrument of historic necessity, Cromwell, who inwardly trembled lest his soul be lost, appears like an introspective character out of a prerevolutionary Russian novel.

Karl Kautsky once characterized Lenin as the Russian Bismarck. In calling attention to the masterly game of revolutionary *Real-Politik* Lenin played, the comparison is apt. But Junker that he was, Bismarck was a divided character. He had no more religion than Napoleon and fancied himself as a kind of Norse hero wresting an empire from the designs of a malignant Fate. Lenin was all of a piece. He created an empire as if it were on order and pretended sincerely that he was merely following out a recipe laid down by Marx and Engels, his holy authorities. A story circulated among the Bolsheviks after his death would have pleased his pious heart. Lenin appeared before the Gates of St. Peter and knocked for admission. "Who are you?" asked St. Peter. To which, instead of giving his name, Lenin modestly replied: "I am the interest on Marx's *Capital.*"

The sense of his historic mission freed Lenin from any shame, embarrassment, and regret in revising his course or in zigzagging from one position to another. He accepted *practical* responsibility, but in his own mind history absolved him from all *moral* responsibility. What would have been utter hypocrisy in a man of little faith appeared in him as flexible intelligence wrestling with the exigencies attendant upon implementing high principle. It is characteristic that those who struggled with him most bitterly in the arena of revolutionary struggle—where no blows or holds are barred—acknowledge his absolute sincerity and his moral force on others. They were fascinated by him even when they most detested him. He wanted nothing for himself—except to determine the destiny of mankind. His judgment could not be swayed by women, friends, or comforts, or tempered by mercy or pity. When Berkman and Goldman pleaded with him to release imprisoned anarchists who had criticized the Bolsheviks, he replied in effect: "Genuine, thinking anar-

chists, agree with us: only bandits posing as anarchists are in jail."
This was monstrously false—but undoubtedly Lenin believed it.
When he advised foreign Communists, introducing Trojan horses
into democratic organizations, to lie about their beliefs and member-
ship, he was firmly convinced that this would be loyalty to a "higher"
truth. When Otto Bauer interpreted the New Economic Policy introduced by Lenin as a partial return to capitalism, Lenin complained,
and with honest indignation: "And the Mensheviks and Social-Revo-
lutionaries, all of whom preach this sort of thing, are astonished
when we say that we will shoot those who say such things." What is
significant here, as elsewhere, is the way Lenin takes it for granted
that the rights of opposition he claimed for himself when he was
out of power are completely without validity when claimed by
others when he is *in* power. . . .

It is to the relatively scant characterizations of Lenin written
while he was still alive that we must go for a reliable account of the
way he impressed the men who worked with him. That is why the
following lines by A. V. Lunacharsky, a keen observer and coworker
of Lenin, are so telling. "Lenin does his work imperiously, not because power is sweet to him, but because he is sure he is right, and
cannot endure to have anybody spoil his work. His love of power
grows out of his tremendous sureness and the correctness of his
principles, and if you please, out of an inability (very useful in a
political leader) to see from the point of view of his opponents."

Pit a man of this "tremendous sureness," imperious will and
drive, organizational genius, and sensitiveness to the psychology of
the crowd against the golden opportunity of national demoralization
following an exhausting war—and the issue of who will rule whom
will never remain long in doubt.

Historians have given considerable—
perhaps too much—attention to notable
figures of the past. While they have
generally not neglected the masses
completely, they have portrayed them
hazily. Moreover, since scholars have
relied heavily on sources written by
articulate leaders, their pictures of the
lower classes often have an elite bias.
JESSE LEMISCH (b. 1936), whose
specialty is American colonial history,
has forcefully urged students of the
past to seek to reinterpret history
"from the bottom up." The following
selection is the introduction and conclusion of an article in which Lemisch
imaginatively examined the viewpoint
of imprisoned merchant seamen during
the American Revolution. Consider
carefully the benefits and problems involved in understanding the "inarticulate."

THE MASSES:
Listening to the "Inarticulate"

"Of kings and gentlemen," wrote W. E. B. Du Bois, "we have the
record ad nause[a]m and in stupid detail. . . ." But of "the common
run of human beings," he went on, "and particularly of the half or
wholly submerged working group, the world has saved all too little
of authentic record and tried to forget or ignore even the little
saved." "Who built the seven towers of Thebes?" echoed Bertolt
Brecht, "The books are filled with names of kings." Such appeals for
what might be called a history of the inarticulate have come not
only from the left, nor have they necessarily been populist in intent.
A century ago, looking at history with somewhat different sym-
pathies, Frederick Law Olmsted, a self-proclaimed "honest growler,"
spoke as much to the question of validity as to that of humanity:

Excerpted from Jesse Lemisch, "Listening to the 'Inarticulate': William Widger's
Dream and the Loyalties of American Revolutionary Seamen in British Prisons,"
Journal of Social History, III (Fall 1969), 1–29. © 1969 by the Regents of the
University of California. Reprinted with permission of the author and the Regents.
Footnotes omitted.

Men of literary taste ... are always apt to overlook the working-classes, and to confine the records they make of their own times, in a great degree, to the habits and fortunes of their own associates, or to those of people of superior rank to themselves, of whose sayings and doings their vanity, as well as their curiosity, leads them to most carefully inform themselves. The dumb masses have often been so lost in this shadow of egotism, that, in later days, it has been impossible to discern the very real influence their character and condition has had on the fortune and fate of nations.

Should the character and condition of the "dumb masses" play a minor role in historiography? *Must* they? The answer to the first question, at least, seems clear: the most conservative standards of evidence and proof require that historiography include a history of the inarticulate. No generalization has much meaning until we have actually examined the constituent parts of the entity about which we are generalizing. No contention about the people on the bottom of a society—neither that they are rebellious nor docile, neither that they defer to an authority whose legitimacy they accept nor that they curse an authority which they deem illegitimate, neither that they are noble nor that they are base—no such contention even approaches being proved until we have in fact attempted a history of the inarticulate. Consensus, in order to demonstrate its validity, must confront the conservative rocks of evidence and sail safely through them, as must any generalization which claims to describe a society on the basis of research on only a part of that society.*

Can we write a history of the inarticulate? It was, in part, to answer that question that I undertook my study of merchant seamen in early America. That study began in dissatisfaction with the role assigned to this group in the secondary literature of the American Revolution. In that literature, seamen appear with great frequency, battling over impressment and rioting in the streets of colonial cities.

---

* Professor Lemisch has elaborated his views on the distortions in the historiography of early America growing out of elitism in his "The American Revolution Seen from the Bottom Up," in Barton J. Bernstein, ed., *Towards a New Past: Dissenting Essays in American History* (New York, 1968), 3–45. See also his "Jack Tar in the Streets: Merchant Seamen in the Politics of Revolutionary America," *William and Mary Quarterly*, 3rd Ser., XXV (1968), 371–407.

But although the accounts suggest that seamen acted consistently against British authority, when historians narrate such events it seems to me that they generally evade their central task—explanation. In the absence of other explanations, it frequently appears that Jack Tar rioted because he is and always has been boisterous and irresponsible, the willing victim of alcoholic fantasies, seeking merely to blow off steam. Or at best the seamen rioted because they were manipulated by certain ill-defined groups.

Even accepting a large role for the accidental and the irrational in human affairs, it seems to me that the job of the historian as social scientist is to limit as much as possible the area within which explanation must rely upon such factors. Manipulation exists and irrationality exists, and the historian must acknowledge them when he finds them. But the historian who would make his discipline a more rigorous one should have as his *working assumption* that human actions are generally purposeful and are related to some system of values as well as needs; given that assumption, it is inadequate for him to "explain" the recurrent conduct of large groups of men who seem to act consistently in accord with certain values by making those groups simply the puppets of their social superiors or the victims of alcohol.

In order to explain the seamen's conduct, I found that I would have to ask of them some of the same kinds of questions which intellectual historians generally ask of an elite: questions concerning loyalties and beliefs, all examined within a context which assumed that Jack Tar, like Thomas Jefferson, had ideas and perhaps something which might be called an ideology. On the track of these ideas, I found that actions which might in themselves appear inexplicable made more sense when causality was explored: the historian decides in advance that Jack Tar is a rebel without cause when he neglects to look for cause. The rioting of the pre-Revolutionary decades, for instance, makes more sense when seen against the background of an ancient and bloody tradition of violent resistance to British authority; impressment, commented a Pennsylvania Revolutionary leader, had produced "an estrangement of the Affections of the People from the Authority" of the British, which had led in turn, "by an easy Progression ... to open Opposition ... and Bloodshed."

I found inadequacies in the approach to the Revolution—primarily from the top down—generally taken by historians. *Of course,*

British officials—insensitive as they were to grievances of the victims of the policies which they administered—could find no better explanation than manipulation for the conduct of the seamen. *Of course,* Admiralty records distorted the realities of impressment, leading those who based their research on such sources to see impressment in the context of a manning problem rather than in the context of deprivation of personal liberty.

The struggle to get inside Jack Tar's head suggested the notion of what might be called an "experimental history." One way of evaluating the contention that a crowd is manipulated is to ask, what would the crowd do in the absence of those alleged to be its manipulators? The social psychologist might devise such a condition, but the historian has no choice but to accept the data provided by the past. As it happens, in the New York Stamp Act riots of 1765, precisely such a condition existed: witnesses who are in conflict on other matters agree that at one point whatever leaders the crowd had had lost control. At this point, eschewing plunder, the crowd (including some four to five hundred seamen) marched some distance in a new direction and in orderly fashion to attack the logical political target. What is of interest to us here is not that in this particular instance a crowd demonstrably had political thoughts of its own but rather that if one attempts to devise conditions under which one might evaluate the thought and conduct of crowds, one may find a historical situation which approximates these conditions.

The notion of an "experimental history" seems crucial for a history of the inarticulate. Given the absence of a laboratory and the impossibility of controlling conditions experimentally, one must sensitize oneself to seek such conditions in the existing data. In effect, the historian of the inarticulate must train himself to think as if he were an experimental social psychologist; he must try to devise experiments for testing various contentions; then he must look to history and do his best to find a "natural experiment"—a situation in which such an experiment was in fact acted out.

* * *

We know what [the merchant seaman] William Widger dreamt sixty thousand nights ago. If we can find William Widger's dream in the published *Historical Collections* of the Essex Institute; if we can find, in Yale's Franklin Collection, rich and poignant letters from seamen which even convey, through their spelling, something of the sound of the spoken language; if Philip Freneau, the man who came to be called "The Poet of the American Revolution," shared some of the experiences of "The British Prison Ship" and wrote of them; if the seamen themselves left us ample materials which invite us to examine their politics, their loyalties, and their culture; if sources such as these and others exist, from which it is possible to construct laboratories in which the inarticulate can be heard—then is it not time that we put "inarticulate" in quotation marks and begin to see the term more as a judgment on the failure of historians than as a description of historiographical reality?

Difficult as it is to ascertain the role of individuals and groups in history, assessing the impact of ideas can prove an even more elusive task. Even when the historian has delineated the dominant ideas of an age, he has difficulty proving that these, rather than other forces, should be given primacy in his explanation of historical changes. Yet ideas do have consequences, and students of the past must be alert to them. RICHARD HOFSTADTER (1916–1970), who has earned great renown for several penetrating and provocative works on American history, here explores the manner in which Darwinian theories of natural selection served in the late nineteenth century to support imperialism and militarism. Does Professor Hofstadter contend that these theories *caused* imperial activity? What special problems are there in attributing a causative role to ideas?

IDEAS: *Racism and Imperialism*

In 1898 the United States waged a three-month war with Spain. It took the Philippine Islands from Spain by treaty and formally annexed the Hawaiian Islands. In 1899 the United States partitioned the Samoan Islands by agreement with Germany, and expressed its policy toward western interests in China in the "Open Door" note. In 1900 Americans took part in suppressing the Chinese Boxer Rebellion. By 1902 the Army had finally suppressed insurrection in the Philippines; and in that year the islands were made an unorganized territory.

As the United States stepped upon the stage of empire, American thought turned once again to the subjects of war and empire; opponents and defenders of expansion and conquest marshaled arguments for their causes. After the fashion of late nineteenth-

From Richard Hofstadter, *Social Darwinism in American Thought* (Boston: Beacon Press, 1955). Copyright © 1944, 1955 by the American Historical Association. Reprinted with permission of the author, the publisher, and the American Historical Association.

century thought, they sought in the world of nature a larger justification for their ideals.

The use of natural selection as a vindication of militarism or imperialism was not new in European or American thought. Imperialists, calling upon Darwinism in defense of the subjugation of weaker races, could point to *The Origin of Species,* which had referred in its subtitle to *The Preservation of Favored Races in the Struggle for Life.* Darwin had been talking about pigeons, but the imperialists saw no reason why his theories should not apply to men, and the whole spirit of the naturalistic world-view seemed to call for a vigorous and unrelenting thoroughness in the application of biological concepts. Had not Darwin himself written complacently in *The Descent of Man* of the likelihood that backward races would disappear before the advance of higher civilizations? Militarists could also point to the harsh fact of the elimination of the unfit as an urgent reason for cultivating the martial virtues and keeping the national powder dry. After the Franco-Prussian War both sides had for the first time invoked Darwinism as an explanation of the facts of battle. "The greatest authority of all the advocates of war is Darwin," explained Max Nordau in the *North American Review* in 1889. "Since the theory of evolution has been promulgated, they can cover their natural barbarism with the name of Darwin and proclaim the sanguinary instincts of their inmost hearts as the last word of science."

It would nevertheless be easy to exaggerate the significance of Darwin for race theory or militarism either in the United States or in western Europe. Neither the philosophy of force nor doctrines of *Machtpolitik* had to wait upon Darwin to make their appearance. Nor was racism strictly a post-Darwinian phenomenon. Gobineau's *Essai sur l'Inégalité des Races Humaines,* a landmark in the history of Aryanism, was published in 1853–55 without benefit of the idea of natural selection. As for the United States, a people long familiar with Indian warfare on the frontier and the pro-slavery arguments of Southern politicians and publicists had been thoroughly grounded in notions of racial superiority. At the time when Darwin was still hesitantly outlining his theory in private, racial destiny had already been called upon by American expansionists to support the conquest of Mexico. "The Mexican race now see in the fate of the aborigines of the north, their own inevitable destiny," an expansionist had written. "They must amalgamate or be lost in the superior vigor of the Anglo-Saxon race, or they must utterly perish."

This Anglo-Saxon dogma became the chief element in American racism in the imperial era; but the *mystique* of Anglo-Saxonism, which for a time had a particularly powerful grip on American historians, did not depend upon Darwinism either for its inception or for its development. It is doubtful that such monuments of English Anglo-Saxon historical writing as Edward Augustus Freeman's *History of the Norman Conquest of England* (1867–79) or Charles Kingsley's *The Roman and the Teuton* (1864) owed much to biology; and certainly John Mitchell Kemble's *The Saxons in England* (1849) was not inspired by the survival of the fittest. Like other varieties of racism, Anglo-Saxonism was a product of modern nationalism and the romantic movement rather than an outgrowth of biological science. Even the idea that a nation is an organism that must either grow or fall into decay, which doubtless received an additional impetus from Darwinism, had been invoked before 1859 by the proponents of "Manifest Destiny."

Still, Darwinism was put in the service of the imperial urge. Although Darwinism was not the primary source of the belligerent ideology and dogmatic racism of the late nineteenth century, it did become a new instrument in the hands of the theorists of race and struggle. The likeness of the Darwinian portrait of nature as a field of battle to the prevailing conceptions of a militant age in which von Moltke could write that "war is an element of the order of the world established by God . . . [without which] the world would stagnate and lose itself in materialism," was too great to escape attention. In the United States, however, such frank and brutal militarism was far less common than a benevolent conception of Anglo-Saxon world domination in the interests of peace and freedom. In the decades after 1885, Anglo-Saxonism, belligerent or pacific, was the dominant abstract rationale of American imperialism.

The Darwinian mood sustained the belief in Anglo-Saxon racial superiority which obsessed many American thinkers in the latter half of the nineteenth century. The measure of world dominion already achieved by the "race" seemed to prove it the fittest. Also, in the 1870's and 1880's many of the historical conceptions of the Anglo-Saxon school began to reflect advances in biology and allied developments in other fields of thought. For a time American historians fell under the spell of the scientific ideal and dreamed of evolving a science of history comparable to the biological sciences. The keynote of their faith could be found in E. A. Freeman's *Comparative Politics* (1874), in which he allied the comparative method with the idea of Anglo-Saxon superiority. "For the purposes of the study of Comparative Politics," he had written, "a political constitution is a specimen to be studied, classified, and labeled, as a building or an animal is studied, classified, and labeled by those to whom buildings or animals are objects of study."

If political constitutions were to be classified and compared by Victorian scholars as if they were animal forms, it was highly probable that the political methods of certain peoples would be favored over others. Inspired by the results of the comparative method in philology and mythology, particularly by the work of Edward Tylor and Max Müller, Freeman tried, using this method, to trace the signs of original unity in the primitive institutions of the Aryans, particularly in the "three most illustrious branches of the common stock—the Greek, the Roman, and the Teuton."

When Herbert Baxter Adams set up his great historical seminar at Johns Hopkins, it was with the official blessing of Freeman; and Freeman's dictum, "History is past politics and politics is present history," was emblazoned on the historical studies that came pouring forth from Adams' seminar. A whole generation of historians receiving their inspiration from the Johns Hopkins school could have said with Henry Adams, "I flung myself obediently into the arms of the Anglo-Saxons in history." The leading notion of the Anglo-Saxon school was that the democratic institutions of England and the United States, particularly the New England town meeting, could be traced back to the primitive institutions of the early German tribes. In spite of differences in detail, the Hopkins historians were in general agreement on their picture of the big, blond, democratic Teuton and on the Teutonic genealogy of self-government. The viewpoint of the school was given a fitting popular expression in 1890 with the publication of James K. Hosmer's *Short History of Anglo-Saxon Freedom,* which drew upon the whole literature of Anglo-Saxondom to establish the thesis that government of the people and by the people is of ancient Anglo-Saxon origin. Wrote Hosmer:

> Though Anglo-Saxon freedom in a more or less partial form has been adopted (it would be better perhaps to say imitated) by every nation in Europe, but Russia, and in Asia by Japan, the hopes for that freedom, in the future, rest with the English-speaking race. By that race

alone it has been preserved amidst a thousand perils; to that race alone is it thoroughly congenial; if we can conceive the possibility of the disappearance among peoples of that race, the chance would be small for that freedom's survival . . .

Hosmer shared the optimism of his English contemporary John Richard Green, who believed that the English-speaking race would grow in enormous numbers and spread over the New World, Africa, and Australia. "The inevitable issue," concluded Hosmer, "is to be that the primacy of the world will lie with us. English institutions, English speech, English thought, are to become the main features of the political, social, and intellectual life of mankind." Thus would the survival of the fittest be written large in the world's political future.

What Hosmer did for Anglo-Saxon history, John W. Burgess did for political theory. His *Political Science and Comparative Constitutional Law,* published in the same year as Hosmer's book, serves as a reminder of German as well as English influences in the American Anglo-Saxon cult; for Burgess, like Herbert Baxter Adams, had received a large part of his graduate training in Germany. The peculiarity of his work, Burgess declared, was its method. "It is a comparative study. It is an attempt to apply the method, which has been found so productive in the domain of Natural Science, to Political Science and Jurisprudence." It was Burgess' contention that political capacity is not a gift common to all nations, but limited to a few. The highest capacity for political organization, he believed, has been shown, in unequal degrees, by the Aryan nations. Of all these, only "the Teuton really dominates the world by his superior political genius."

It is therefore not to be assumed that every nation must become a state. The political subjection or attachment of unpolitical nations to those possessing political endowment appears, if we may judge from history, to be as truly a part of the world's civilization as is the national organization of states. I do not think that Asia and Africa can ever receive political organization in any other way. . . . The national state is . . . the most modern and complete solution of the whole problem of political organization which the world has yet produced; and the fact that it is the creation of Teutonic political genius stamps the Teutonic nations as the political nations *par excellence*, and authorizes them, in the economy of the world, to assume the leadership in the establishment and administration of states. . . . The Teutonic nations can never regard the exercise of political power as a right of man. With them this power must be based upon capacity to discharge political duty, and they themselves are the best organs which have as yet appeared to determine when and where this capacity exists.

Theodore Roosevelt, who had been Burgess' student at Columbia Law School was also inspired by the drama of racial expansion. In his historical work, *The Winning of the West*, Roosevelt drew from the story of the frontiersman's struggle with the Indians the conclusion that the coming of the whites was not to be stayed and a racial war to the finish was inevitable. "During the past three centuries," wrote the young scholar-in-politics, "the spread of the English-speaking peoples over the world's waste spaces has been not only the most striking feature in the world's history, but also the event of all others most far-reaching in its effects and its importance." This great expansion he traced back many centuries to the days when German tribes went forth to conquest from their marshy forests. American development represents the culminating achievement of this mighty history of racial growth.

The writings of John Fiske, one of the earliest American synthesizers of evolutionism, expansionism, and the Anglo-Saxon myth, show how tenuous could be the boundary between Spencer's ideal evolutionary pacifism and the militant imperialism which succeeded it. A kindly man, whose thought was grounded in Spencer's theory of the transition from militancy to industrialism, Fiske was not the sort to advocate violence as an instrument of national policy. Yet even in his hands evolutionary dogma issued forth in a bumptious doctrine of racial destiny. In his *Outlines of Cosmic Philosophy*, Fiske had followed Spencer in accepting the universality of conflict (outside of family relationships) as a fact in savage society; he believed it an effective agent in selection. But the superior, more differentiated and integrated societies had come to prevail over the more backward by natural selection, and the power of making war on a grand scale had become concentrated in the hands of "those communities in which predatory activity is at the minimum and industrial activity at the maximum." So warfare or destructive competition gives place to the productive competition of industrial society. As militancy declines, the method of conquest is replaced by the method of federation.

Fiske, who had long believed in Aryan race superiority, also accepted the "Teutonic" theory of democracy. This doctrine sanctified any conquest incidental to Anglo-Saxon expansion. English victories over France in the eighteenth-century colonial struggles represented a victory for industrialism over militancy. The American victory over Spain and the acquisition of the Philippines Fiske interpreted as the high point in a conflict between Spanish colonization and superior English methods.

In 1880, when he was invited to speak before the Royal Institute of Great Britain, Fiske gave a series of three lectures on "American Political Ideas" which became widely known as a statement of the Anglo-Saxon thesis. Fiske praised the ancient Roman Empire as an agency of peace, but argued that it had been inadequate as a system of political organization because it failed to combine concerted action with local self-government. The solution to this ancient need could be provided by representative democracy and the local self-government embodied in the New England town. By retaining the rustic democracy of America's Aryan forefathers, American federal organization would make possible an effective union of many diverse states. Democracy, diversity, and peace would be brought into harmony. The dispersion of this magnificent Aryan political system over the world, and the complete elimination of warfare, was the next step in world history.

With characteristic Darwinian emphasis upon race fertility, Fiske dwelt upon the great population potential of the English and American races. America could support at least 700,000,000; and the English people would within a few centuries cover Africa with teeming cities, flourishing farms, railroads, telegraphs, and all the devices of civilization. This was the Manifest Destiny of the race. Every land on the globe that was not already the seat of an old civilization should become English in language, traditions, and blood. Four-fifths of the human race would trace its pedigree to

English forefathers. Spread from the rising to the setting sun, the race would hold the sovereignty of the sea and the commercial supremacy which it had begun to acquire when England first began to settle the New World. If the United States would only drop its shameful tariff and enter into free competition with the rest of the world, it would exert such pressure, peacefully of course, that the states of Europe would no longer be able to afford armaments and would finally see the advantages of peace and federation. Thus, according to Fiske, would man finally pass out of barbarism and become truly Christian.

Even Fiske, who was accustomed to platform success, was astonished at the enthusiasm evoked by these addresses in England and at home. The lecture on "Manifest Destiny," published in *Harper's* in 1885, was repeated more than twenty times in cities throughout the United States. By request of President Hayes, Chief Justice Waite, Senators Hoar and Dawes of Massachusetts, General Sherman, George Bancroft, and others, Fiske gave his lectures again at Washington, where he was feted by the politicos and presented to the Cabinet.

As a spokesman of expansion, however, Fiske was but a small voice compared with the Rev. Josiah Strong, whose book *Our Country: Its Possible Future and Its Present Crisis*, appeared in 1885 and soon sold 175,000 copies in English alone. Strong, then secretary of the Evangelical Society of the United States, wrote the book primarily to solicit money for missions. His uncanny capacity for assimilating the writings of Darwin and Spencer to the prejudices of rural Protestant America makes the book one of the most revealing documents of its time. Strong exulted in the material resources of the United States, but he was dissatisfied with its spiritual life. He was against immigrants, Catholics, Mormons, saloons, tobacco, large cities, socialists, and concentrated wealth—all grave menaces to the Republic. Still he was undaunted in his faith in universal progress, material and moral, and the future of the Anglo-Saxon race. He employed the economic argument for imperialism; and a decade before Frederick Jackson Turner he saw in the imminent exhaustion of the public lands a turning point in national development. It was Anglo-Saxonism, however, that brought him to the highest pitch of enthusiasm. The Anglo-Saxon people, the bearers of civil liberty and pure spiritual Christianity, said Strong,

140

. . . is multiplying more rapidly than any other European race. It already owns one-third of the earth, and will get more as it grows. By 1980 the world Anglo-Saxon race should number at least 713,000,000. Since North America is much bigger than the little English isle, it will be the seat of Anglo-Saxondom.

If human progress follows a law of development, if "Time's noblest offspring is the last," our civilization should be the noblest; for we are "The heirs of all the ages in the foremost files of time," and not only do we occupy the latitude of power, but *our land is the last to be occupied in that latitude.* There is no other virgin soil in the North Temperate Zone. If the consummation of human progress is not to be looked for here, if there is yet to flower a higher civilization, where is the soil that is to produce it?

Strong went on to show how a new and finer physical type was emerging in the United States, bigger, stronger, taller than Scots or Englishmen. Darwin himself, Strong noted triumphantly, had seen in the superior vigor of Americans an illustration of natural selection at work, when he wrote in *The Descent of Man:*

There is apparently much truth in the belief that the wonderful progress of the United States, as well as the character of the people, are the results of natural selection; for the more energetic, restless, and courageous men from all parts of Europe have emigrated during the last ten or twelve generations to that great country, and have there succeeded best. Looking to the distant future, I do not think that the Reverend Mr. Zincke takes an exaggerated view when he says: "All other series of events—as that which resulted in the culture of mind in Greece, and that which resulted in the empire of Rome— only appear to have purpose and value when viewed in connection with, or rather as subsidiary to . . . the great stream of Anglo-Saxon emigration to the west."

Returning to his theme that the unoccupied lands of the world were filling up, and that population would soon be pressing upon subsistence in the United States as in Europe and Asia, Strong declared:

> Then will the world enter upon a new stage of its history—*the final competition of races for which the Anglo-Saxon is being schooled.* If I do not read amiss, this powerful race will move down upon Mexico, down upon Central and South America, out upon the islands of the sea, over upon Africa and beyond. And can anyone doubt that the result of this competition of races will be the "survival of the fittest"?

Although concrete economic and strategic interests, such as Chinese trade and the vital necessity of sea power, were the prominent issues in the imperial debate, the movement took its rationale from more general ideological conceptions. The appeal of Anglo-Saxonism was reflected in the adherence to it of political leaders of the expansion movement. The idea of inevitable Anglo-Saxon destiny figured in the outlook of Senators Albert J. Beveridge and Henry Cabot Lodge and of John Hay, Theodore Roosevelt's Secretary of State, as well as the President himself. During the fight for the annexation of the Philippines, when the larger question of imperial policy was thrown open for debate, expansionists were quick to invoke the law of progress, the inevitable tendency to expand, the Manifest Destiny of Anglo-Saxons, and the survival of the fittest. Before the Senate in 1899, Beveridge cried:

> God has not been preparing the English-speaking and Teutonic peoples for a thousand years for nothing but vain and idle self-admiration. No! He has made us the master organizers of the world to establish system where chaos reigns. . . . He has made us adepts in government that we may administer government among savages and senile peoples.

In the most memorable of his imperialist exhortations, "The Strenuous Life" (1899), Theodore Roosevelt warned of the possibility of national elimination in the international struggle for existence:

142

We cannot avoid the responsibilities that confront us in Hawaii, Cuba, Porto Rico, and the Philippines. All we can decide is whether we shall meet them in a way that will redound to the national credit, or whether we shall make of our dealings with these new problems a dark and shameful page in our history. . . . The timid man, the lazy man, the man who distrusts his country, the over-civilized man, who has lost the great fighting, masterful virtues, the ignorant man, and the man of dull mind, whose soul is incapable of feeling the mighty lift that thrills "stern men with empires in their brains"— all these, of course, shrink from seeing the nation undertake its new duties. . . .

I preach to you, then, my countrymen, that our country calls not for the life of ease but for the life of strenuous endeavor. The twentieth century looms before us big with the fate of many nations. If we stand idly by, if we seek merely swollen, slothful ease and ignoble peace, if we shrink from the hard contests where men must win at hazard of their lives and at the risk of all they hold dear, then the bolder and stronger peoples will pass us by, and will win for themselves the domination of the world.

John Hay found in the impulse to expand a sign of an irresistible "cosmic tendency." "No man, no party, can fight with any chance of final success against a cosmic tendency; no cleverness, no popularity avails against the spirit of the age." "If history teaches any lesson," echoed another writer a few years later, "it is that nations, like individuals, follow the law of their being; that in their growth and in their decline they are creatures of conditions in which their own volition plays but a part, and that often the smallest part." The question of the Philippines was sometimes pictured as the watershed of American destiny; our decision would determine whether we should undergo a new expansion greater than any in the past, or fall back into decline as a senile people. Said John Barrett, former minister to Siam:

Now is the critical time when the United States should strain every nerve and bend all her energies to keep well in front in the mighty struggle that has begun for the supremacy of the Pacific Seas. If we seize the opportunity we may become leaders forever, but if we are laggards now we will remain laggards until the crack of doom. The rule of the survival of the fittest applies to nations as well as to the animal kingdom. It is a cruel, relentless principle being exercised in a cruel, relentless competition of mighty forces; and these will trample over us without sympathy or remorse unless we are trained to endure and strong enough to stand the pace.

Charles A. Conant, a prominent journalist and economist troubled about the necessity of finding an outlet for surplus capital, "if the entire fabric of the present economic order is not to be shaken by a social revolution," argued that

> ... the law of self-preservation, as well as that of the survival of the fittest, is urging our people on in a path which is undoubtedly a departure from the policy of the past, but which is inevitably marked out by the new conditions and requirements of the present.

Conant warned against the possibility of decadence if the country did not seize upon its opportunities at once. Another writer denied that a policy of colonial expansion was anything novel in American history. We had colonized the West. The question was not whether we should now enter upon a colonial career but whether we should shift our colonizing heritage into new channels. "We must not forget that the Anglo-Saxon race is expansive."

Although the Anglo-Saxon *mystique* was called upon in the interests of expansion by might, it also had its more pacific side. Its devotees had usually recognized a powerful bond with England; the historians of the Anglo-Saxon school, stressing the common political heritage, wrote about the American Revolution as if it were a temporary misunderstanding in a long history of common political evolution, or a welcome stimulant to flagging Anglo-Saxon liberties.

One outgrowth of the Anglo-Saxon legend was a movement toward an Anglo-American alliance which came to rapid fruition in the closing years of the nineteenth century. In spite of its un-

144

flagging conviction of racial superiority, this movement was peaceful rather than militaristic in its motivation; for its followers generally believed that an Anglo-American understanding, alliance, or federation would usher in a "golden age" of universal peace and freedom. No possible power or combination of powers would be strong enough to challenge such a union. This "English-speaking people's league of God for the permanent peace of this war-worn world," as Senator Beveridge called it, would be the next stage in the world's evolution. Advocates of Anglo-American unity believed that Spencer's transition from militant to pacific culture, and Tennyson's "Parliament of Man, the Federation of the World," were about to become a reality.

James K. Hosmer had appealed in 1890 for an "English-Speaking Fraternity" powerful enough to withstand any challenge by the Slavs, Hindus, or Chinese. This coalescence of like-minded states would be but the first step toward a brotherhood of humanity. Yet it was not until 1897 that American interest in an English alliance resulted in a movement of consequence, which received the support of publicists and statesmen as well as littérateurs and historians. During the war with Spain, when continental nations took a predominantly hostile attitude toward American interests, Britain's friendliness stood out in welcome relief. Common fears of Russia and a feeling of identity of interests in the Far East were added to the notion of a common racial destiny. The Anglophobia which had been so persistent among American politicians—Roosevelt and Lodge had been among the bitterest—was considerably relieved. The anti-imperialist Carl Schurz felt that what he rather prematurely took to be the complete dissipation of anti-English feeling was one of the best results of the Spanish-American War. Richard Olney—who as Cleveland's Secretary of State during the Venezuela dispute had defiantly told Britain that the fiat of the United States is law in the Western Hemisphere—now wrote an article on "The International Isolation of the United States" to point out the benefits of British trade and to warn against pursuing an anti-British policy at a time when our country stood alone in the world. Arguing that "family quarrels" were a thing of the past, Olney expressed his hope for Anglo-American diplomatic cooperation, and reminded his readers: "There is a patriotism of race as well as of country." Even the navalist Mahan approved of the British, and although he had felt for some time that a movement for union was premature, he was sufficiently friendly to be content to let the British retain naval supremacy. For a short time at the close of the century the Anglo-Saxon movement became the rage among the upper classes, and statesmen spoke seriously of a possible political alliance.

The Anglo-Saxon cult, however, had to pull against the great mass of the population, whose ethnic composition and cultural background rendered them immune to its propaganda; and even among those of Anglo-Saxon lineage the dynamic appeal of the cult was confined to the years of excitement at the turn of the century. The term "Anglo-Saxon" offended many people, and meetings of protest against Anglo-Saxonism were called in some of the western states. Suspicion of England, traditional in American politics, could not be overcome. John Hay complained in 1900 of "a mad-dog hatred of England prevalent among newspapers and politicians." When the movement for Anglo-American Union was revived again during the First World War, the term "English-speaking" was used in preference to "Anglo-Saxon," and racial exclusiveness was no longer featured. The powerful undertow of American isolation that followed the war, however, swept away this movement once again.

Anglo-Saxonism in politics was limited both in scope and in duration. It had its day of influence as a doctrine of national self-assertion, but as a doctrine of Anglo-Saxon world order its effects were ephemeral. Even the benevolent ideal of the dreamers of a Pax Anglo-Americana found practical meaning only as a timely justification of a temporary rapprochement inspired by the needs of *Realpolitik*. The day had not come when world peace could be imposed by a "superior" race confident in its biological blessings and its divine mission.

Lacking an influential military caste, the United States never developed a strong military cult audacious enough to glorify war for its own sake. Such outbursts as Roosevelt's "Strenuous Life" speech were rare; and it was also rare for an American writer to extol war for its effects upon the race, although Rear Admiral Stephen B. Luce, one of Mahan's patrons, once declared that war is one of the great agencies of human conflict and that "strife in one form or another in the organic world seems to be the law of existence. . . . Suspend the struggle, well called the battle of life, for a brief space, and death claims the victory." Most writers on war seemed to agree with Spencer that military conflict had been highly useful in developing primitive civilization but had now long outlived its value as an instrument of progress.

The advocates of preparedness did not usually take the stand that there is anything inherently desirable in war, but rather quoted the old maxim, "If you wish for peace, prepare for war." "Let us worship peace, indeed," conceded Mahan, "as the goal at which humanity must hope to arrive; but let us not fancy that peace is to be had as a boy wrenches an unripe fruit from a tree."

Others took the position that strife is inherent in the nature of things and must be anticipated as an unhappy necessity. Once the martial fever of the short and easy war with Spain had subsided, the psychology of the American people between 1898 and 1917 was surprisingly nervous and defensive for a nation that was rapidly rising in stature as a world power. Encouraged by the eugenics movement, men talked of racial degeneracy, of race suicide, of the decline of western civilization, of the effeteness of the western peoples, of the Yellow Peril. Warnings of decay were most commonly coupled with exhortations to revivify the national spirit.

One of the most popular among the pessimistic writers was an Englishman, Charles Pearson, who had formerly served the Empire as minister of education in Victoria. His melancholy book, *National Life and Character*, published in England and the United States in 1893, offered a discouraging prognosis for western culture. The higher races, Pearson believed, can live only in the temperate zone, and will be forever barred from effective colonization in the tropics. Overpopulation and economic exigencies will give rise to state socialism, which will extend its tentacles into every corner of western national life. Because of the increasing dependence of the citizen upon the state, nationalism will grow, and religion, family life, and old-fashioned morality will decline. There will also be a consolidation of peoples into great centralized empires, for only these will have the capacity to survive. Large armies, great cities, huge national debts will hasten cultural eclipse. The decline of competition, coupled with state education, will render the intellect more mechanical in its operations and deprive it of the initiative that alone is capable of outstanding achievement in the arts. The result will be a world of old people, scientific rather than esthetic, unprogressive, stable, without adventure, energy, brightness, hope, or ambition. Meanwhile other races will not fail in vitality, for biology shows that the lower are more prolific than the higher.

147

Chinese, Hindus, Negroes cannot be exterminated, but will on the contrary be likely to challenge the supremacy of western civilization by industrial rather than military means. Perhaps the best that the governing races can do is to face the future with courage and dignity.

> It is idle to say that if all this should come to pass our pride of place will not be humiliated. We were struggling among ourselves for supremacy in a world which we thought of as destined to belong to the Aryan races and to the Christian faith; to the letters and arts and charm of social manners which we have inherited from the best times of the past. We shall wake to find ourselves elbowed and hustled, and perhaps even thrust aside by peoples whom we looked down upon as servile, and thought of as bound always to minister to our needs. The solitary consolation will be that the changes have been inevitable. It has been our work to organize and create, to carry peace and law and order over the world, that others may enter in and enjoy. Yet in some of us the feeling of caste is so strong that we are not sorry to think we shall have passed away before that day arrives.

Pearson's fears were the beginning of a reaction from the optimism expressed by Fiske and Strong in the 1880's. For middle-class intellectuals, reeling under the shock of the panic of 1893 and the deep social discontents of the prolonged depression that followed, his prophecies of doom had a ring of truth. They were particularly suited to the dark mood that overcame Henry Adams in the 1890's. He wrote to C. M. Gaskell:

> I am satisfied that Pearson is right, and that the dark races are gaining on us, as they have already done in Haiti, and are doing throughout the West Indies and our Southern States. In another fifty years, at the same rate of movement, the white races will have to reconquer the tropics by war and nomadic invasion, or be shut up, north of the fortieth parallel.

To his brother, Brooks Adams, pessimism was more than a matter of private despair. In his study of *The Law of Civilization and Decay* (1896), he set forth his own version of the deeper historical principles behind the façade of social change. The law of force and energy is universal, said Adams in a passage somewhat reminiscent of Spencer, and animal life is only one of the outlets through which solar energy is dissipated. Human societies are forms of animal life, differing in energy according to their natural endowments; but all societies obey the general law that the social movement of a community is proportionate to its energy and mass, and that its degree of centralization is proportionate to its mass. The surplus energetic material not expended by a society in the daily struggle for life can be stored as wealth, and the stored energy is transmitted from one community to another either by conquest or by superiority in economic competition. Every race sooner or later reaches the limit of its warlike energy and enters upon a phase of economic competition. Surplus energy, when accumulated in such bulk as to preponderate over productive energy, becomes the controlling social force. Capital becomes autocratic. The economic and scientific intellect grows at the expense of imaginative, emotional, and martial arts. A stationary period may supervene, lasting until it is terminated by war or exhaustion or both.

> The evidence, however, seems to point to the conclusion that, when a highly centralized society disintegrates, under the pressure of economic competition, it is because the energy of the race has been exhausted. Consequently, the survivors of such a community lack the power necessary for renewed concentration, and must probably remain inert until supplied with fresh energetic material by the infusion of barbarian blood.

In subsequent volumes, *America's Economic Supremacy* (1900) and *The New Empire* (1902), Adams worked out a materialistic interpretation of society based upon physics, biology, geography, and economics. Surveying the rise and decline of historic states, he attributed changes in supremacy to changes in basic trade routes. The center of economic civilization, now once again in transit, he saw coming to rest in the United States; but he warned that "supremacy has always entailed its sacrifices as well as its triumphs, and fortune has seldom smiled on those who, beside being energetic and industrious, have not been armed, organized, and bold."

Nature tends to favor organisms that operate most cheaply—that is, with the most economic expenditure of energy. Wasteful organisms are rejected by nature; they can be eliminated by commerce if not by conquest. Adams was particularly anxious about a possible conflict with Russia in the east, for which he thought the United States should be well armed. Concerning the tendency toward centralized empires, he wrote:

> Moreover, Americans must recognize that this is war to the death—a struggle no longer against single nations but against a continent. There is not room in the economy of the world for two centres of wealth and empire. One organism, in the end, will destroy the other. The weaker must succumb. Under commercial competition, that society will survive which works cheapest; but to be undersold is often more fatal to a population than to be conquered.

More influential than Brooks Adams was Captain Alfred Thayer Mahan, whose book *The Influence of Sea Power upon History* (1890) had made him the world's most prominent exponent of navalism. In *The Interest of America in Sea Power* (1897), in which he urged that the country pursue a stronger policy than the present one of "passive self-defense," Mahan pointed out:

> All around us now is strife; "the struggle of life," "the race of life," are phrases so familiar that we do not feel their significance till we stop to think about them. Everywhere nation is arrayed against nation; our own no less than others.

Theodore Roosevelt was among those who tried to stir the nation against the eventualities predicted by Pearson and foreseen by Brooks Adams. For Pearson's pessimism he saw little excuse; although he conceded that civilized nations were not destined to rule the tropics, he could not believe that the white races would lose heart or become intimidated by the tropic races. When western institutions, and democratic government itself, spread to the tropics, the danger of an overpowering industrial competition would be considerably less; and it seemed unlikely that high industrial efficiency would be achieved without a marked degree of westernization. He was somewhat more favorably impressed with the work of his friend Brooks Adams, but again the most pessimistic prophecies aroused Roosevelt to reply. He did not believe that the martial type of man necessarily decays as civilization progresses; pointing to the examples of Russia and Spain, he argued that the phenomenon of national decline should not be too closely identified with advancing industrialism. Only when Adams mentioned the failure to produce enough healthy children did he touch upon the real danger to our society. This was a theme dear to Roosevelt's heart. Vociferously fearful of the menace of race decadence through decline in the birth rate, he never tired of the theme of reproduction and motherhood. If marriages did not produce an average of four children, the numbers of the race could not be maintained. He warned that if the process of racial decay continued in the United States and the British Empire, the future of the white race would rest in the hands of the German and the Slav.

Associated with fears of racial decline and of the loss of fighting fiber was the menace of the Yellow Peril, which was much talked about between 1905 and 1916. The prevailing western attitude toward Japan had been friendly until the Japanese victory over Russia in 1905. However, with the convincing demonstration of the Japanese martial prowess, attitudes changed, just as they had toward Germany after her victory in 1871. In the United States, fear of the Japanese was especially strong in California, where oriental immigration had been resented for over thirty years. The sensational press took up the Japanese menace and exploited it to the point of stimulating occasional war scares.

In 1904 Jack London, always a strenuous advocate of racial assertiveness, warned in an article in the *San Francisco Examiner* of the potential threat to the Anglo-Saxon world if the organizing and ruling capacities of the Japanese should ever gain control of the enormous working capacity of the great Chinese population. The impending racial conflict, he thought, might come to a head in his own time.

> The possibility of race adventure has not passed away. We are in the midst of our own. The Slav is just girding himself up to begin. Why may not the yellow and brown start out on an adventure as tremendous as our own and more strikingly unique?

Hugh H. Lusk believed that the Japanese menace was only a small part of a general reawakening of the Mongolian race, whose urge to expansion, motivated by the age-old population problem, might soon send it out over the Pacific and ultimately to south-western America and to the gates of the United States via Mexico. Talk of the Yellow Peril reached its height just before the First World War, when congressmen spoke openly of inevitable conflict in the Pacific.

Perhaps the closest American approximation to the German militarist writer General von Bernhardi was General Homer Lea, a colorful military adventurer who fought against the Boxer Rebellion, and later became an adviser to Sun Yat-sen. Lea's militarism was based directly upon biology. He believed that nations are like organisms in their dependence upon growth and expansion to resist disease and decay.

> As physical vigor represents the strength of man in his struggle for existence, in the same sense military vigor constitutes the strength of nations; ideals, laws and constitutions are but temporary effulgences, and are existent only so long as this strength remains vital. As manhood marks the height of physical vigor among mankind, so the militant successes of a nation mark the zenith of its physical greatness.

Militancy may be divided into three phases: the militancy of the struggle to survive, the militancy of conquest, and the militancy of supremacy or preservation of ownership. It is in the first stage, the struggle to survive, that the genius of a people reaches its height; the harder this struggle, the more highly developed is the military spirit, with the result that conquerors often arise from desolate wastes or rocky islands. The laws of struggle and survival are universal and unalterable, and the duration of national existence is dependent upon the knowledge of them.

> Plans to thwart them, to short-cut them, circumvent, to cozen, to scorn and violate [them] is folly such as man's conceit alone makes possible. Never has this been tried —and man is ever at it—but what the end has been gangrenous and fatal.

Lea warned of the possibility of Japanese invasion of the United States, and argued that a war with Japan would be settled by land campaigns, for which the country needed a much larger army. Without such a military establishment, the West Coast would stand in deadly danger of invasion. The strategy of such an invasion Lea had planned in full detail.

Lea further warned that the Saxon races were flouting the laws of nature by permitting the militancy of their people to decline. A decadent tendency to let individual wants take precedence over the necessities of national existence threatened Anglo-Saxon power throughout the world, he believed. The United States, submerged by a flood of non-Anglo-Saxon immigrants, was ceasing to be the stronghold of a Saxon race. The British Empire was in serious danger from the colored races. The day of the Saxon was ending. For the impending struggle between the Germans and the Saxon race, the latter was ill equipped. There was only one antidote for Anglo-Saxon decline: greater militancy. A confederation would be weak in war, but universal compulsory military service might check the already alarming decline.

The advocates of preparedness made a biological appeal similar to Lea's. Hudson Maxim, an inventor of smokeless powder, and brother of Hiram Maxim, the inventor of the Maxim gun, published a volume called *Defenseless America* (1914), which was widely distributed by Hearst's International Library. "Self-preservation," Maxim warned, "is the first law of Nature, and this law applies to nations exactly as it applies to individuals. Our American Republic cannot survive unless it obeys the law of survival." He argued that man is by nature a struggling animal, that human nature has always been more or less the same. To be unprepared for the struggle would be to risk extinction, but preparedness might avert war.

A similar philosophy could be found among the wartime leaders of the organized preparedness movement. S. Stanwood Menken, chairman of the National Security League's Congress of Constructive Patriotism, warned the delegates that the law of the survival of the fittest applied to nations, and that the United States could assert its fitness only through a national reawakening. General Leonard Wood was skeptical of the possibility of suppressing war, which, he said, "is about as difficult as to effectively neutralize the general law which governs all things, namely the survival of the fittest." Although the biological argument for militarism was hardly the dominant note among American leaders, it did give them a cosmic foundation that appealed to a Darwinized national mentality.

BIBLIOGRAPHY

The following is a highly selective list of recommended books on the nature of history. Although by no means unsophisticated, they have the virtue of being written in non-technical language suitable for undergraduate reading at all levels. All are available in paperback editions.

Barzun, Jacques, and Henry F. Graff. *The Modern Researcher*. rev. ed. New York: Harcourt, Brace, 1970.

Becker, Carl L. *Everyman His Own Historian*. New York: Crofts, 1935.

Bloch, Marc. *The Historian's Craft*. New York: Knopf, 1953.

Carr, Edward H. *What is History?* New York: Knopf, 1962.

Commager, Henry S. *The Study of History*. Columbus, Ohio: Charles E. Merrill, 1966.

Gottschalk, Louis. *Understanding History*. 2d ed. New York: Knopf, 1969.

Gustavson, Carl G. *A Preface to History*. New York: McGraw-Hill, 1955.

Hook, Sidney. *The Hero in History*. New York: Humanities Press, 1943.

Kitson Clark, G. *The Critical Historian*. London: Heinemann Educational Books, 1967.

Marwick, Arthur. *The Nature of History*. London: Macmillan, 1970.

Nevins, Allan. *The Gateway to History*. rev. ed. Garden City, N.Y.: Doubleday, 1962.

Stern, Fritz (ed.). *The Varieties of History*. Cleveland: Meridian Books, 1957.

Walsh, W. H. *An Introduction to the Philosophy of History*. London: Hutchinson's Universal Library, 1950.

INDEX

new insights to past, 55; capacity of, for good or evil, 8–11; as chronicler of own times, 74; as "cliometrician," 43; components of his prowess, 20; as custodian of memories and dreams, 78; detachment as goal of, 21, 36–37, 65–66; effect of experiences on work, 20, 38–40, 53–54, 56–60, 63–64, 66–67; as "history-minded," 51–64 *passim;* as individual human being, 15, 20, 38–40, 56–58, 64; as instrument, 36–37; methodological conservatism of, 41–42; obligation of, to future, 26–27; over-certainty of, 67–70; as "present-minded," 51–64 *passim;* and presentation of alternative courses of action, 74–75, 77–78; as product of his day, 51–64; radical, 21, 73, 76–77; as "relativist," 20, 29–40; as scientist, 19–20, 23–27, 36; seeking truth, 24; selectivity of, 38

Historical forces, 81–82; economic, 91–102; intellectual, 133–153; leaders ("great men") as, 115–126; "inarticulate" as, 127–131; political, 83–90; social, 91–102; wars as, 103–114

History: ambiguity of term, 36, 65; causation in, 81–82; as concern of all men, 3–5, 16–18; controversy over nature of, 19–21, 21–79 *passim;* diverse interpretations of, 21, 38–40, 54–55, 62–64; effects of, on word meanings, 8–10; as escape from immediate environment, 4, 25–26, 59–60; "experimental," 130; futility of ignoring, 11–12; ingredients of, 81–153 *passim;* nature of facts in, 29–40; obscure patterns in, 67–70; pervasive influence of, 7–8; place of, in higher education, 26; pleasure in studying, 4; and policy-making, 4, 8–9, 71, 74–75; as presenting forgotten

alternatives, 74; propagandistic uses of, 10–11; providing collective past, 78; quantitative components of, 41–48; radical, 21, 73–79; relevance of, 3–5, 8–12, 25–27; and resolution of perplexities, 4; scientific, 19–20, 23–27, 36; and shaping of human development, 25–26, 71; social, 46–50; as source of consolation, 4. *See also:* Historian; Historical forces; Interpretation, historical

Hofstadter, Richard, 132; on racism and imperialism, 133–153

Hook, Sidney, 82, 115; on hero in history, 115–126

Interpretation, historical: balance in, 82; computer as aid to, 41–44, 46–50; dangers of oversimplifying, 67–70; emphasis of, on leaders, 115–126, 127–128; human element in, 15, 20, 36–40; limitations by factual framework, 63–64; neglect of "inarticulate" in, 127–131; reasons for changes in, 21, 38–40, 54–55; as weighing of diverse elements, 81–82. *See also* Causation

Kitson Clark, George, 4, 7; on critical historian, 7–18

Koht, Halvdan, 83; on advancing power of state, 83–90

Lefebvre de Noëttes, 54–55

Lemisch, Jesse, 82, 87; on listening to "inarticulate," 127–131

Lippmann, Walter, 65–66

Lynd, Staughton, 21, 73; on historical past and existential present, 73–79

Macaulay, Thomas B., 66–67

Maitland, F. W., 5

Marshall, George, 69

Marx, Karl, 73, 81

PRINTED IN U.S.A.